T0303245

THE MESSAGE

THE MESSAGE
Your Secrets in the Cards

By Deborah Leigh

BOOKS

Winchester, U.K.
New York, U.S.A.

First published by O Books, 2008
O Books is an imprint of John Hunt Publishing
Ltd., The Bothy, Deershot Lodge, Park Lane,
Ropley, Hants, SO24 0BE, UK
office1@o-books.net
www.o-books.net

Distribution in:

UK and Europe
Orca Book Services
orders@orcabookservices.co.uk
Tel: 01202 665432 Fax: 01202 666219 Int.
code (44)

USA and Canada
NBN
custserv@nbnbooks.com
Tel: 1 800 462 6420 Fax: 1 800 338 4550

Australia and New Zealand
Brumby Books
sales@brumbybooks.com.au
Tel: 61 3 9761 5535 Fax: 61 3 9761 7095

Far East (offices in Singapore, Thailand, Hong
Kong, Taiwan)
Pansing Distribution Pte Ltd
kemal@pansing.com
Tel: 65 6319 9939 Fax: 65 6462 5761

South Africa
Alternative Books
altbook@peterhyde.co.za
Tel: 021 555 4027 Fax: 021 447 1430

Text copyright Deborah Leigh 2008

Design: Jim Weaver

ISBN: 978 1 84694 095 8

All rights reserved. Except for brief
quotations in critical articles or reviews, no
part of this book may be reproduced in any
manner without prior written permission
from the publishers.

The rights of Deborah Leigh as author
have been asserted in accordance with the
Copyright, Designs and Patents Act 1988.

A CIP catalogue record for this book is
available from the British Library.

Printed in the US by Maple Vail

O Books operates a distinctive and ethical publishing philosophy in
all areas of its business, from its global network of authors to
production and worldwide distribution.

No trees were cut down to print this particular book. The paper is
100% recycled, with 50% of that being post-consumer. It's processed
chlorine-free, and has no fibre from ancient or endangered forests.
This production method on this print run saved approx. 13 trees,
4,000 gallons of water, 600 pounds of solid waste, 990 pounds of
greenhouse gases and 8 million Btu of energy. On its publication a
tree was planted in a new forest that O Books is sponsoring at The
Village www.thefourgates.com

Dedication

To Thomas and Barbie who inspired me
and Daryl who made it happen.

Table of Contents

From The Author

Personal Prophesy is a system of intuitively living your life and I learned the fundamentals of this from my maternal grandmother. It seems incredible that few in my family were aware that she had the ability to read playing cards. It wasn't until 1980 that she introduced me to Personal Prophesy and began teaching me how to read cards for myself, until her death in 1982.

My grandmother was not a well-educated woman. She never finished high school. She never had a professional career. Still, she was wise beyond her years and truly had a genius for founding this method of intuitively living your life.

I have furthered the study of Personal Prophesy since her death and find it most rewarding to teach others to intuitively find their lives in a deck of ordinary playing cards.

The success rate I've experienced with this method over the years has been phenomenal. It has:

- Given inspiration and meaning to the lives of countless individuals
- Brought soulmates together from around the world
- Inspired spiritual visions
- Forecast important world events
- Prepared individuals for serious personal tragedy
- Prevented impending suicides

- Provided solid career advances and enabled law students to pass the Bar Exam
- Cured bulimia
- Prevented the termination of a pregnancy deemed by medical specialists to be genetically defective

In the 25 years that I have spent reading cards for the public and teaching others how to read cards for themselves, my primary goal has always been to bring people to the realization that the message of the cards is primarily an intuitive experience in discovery, one that belongs to each of us individually.

The more we develop the perception we are using to assist us in that discovery, the more life-enriching the experience becomes. Yet, no matter how much we may actually know about what causes us to accurately perceive the future, there is always more to learn.

When you commit yourself to the task of reading cards fluently and frequently, you never stop learning. I'm convinced that is the main fascination surrounding this skill. There is never an end to the story the cards have to tell, regardless of who we are or the walks of life we come from.

Over the past two decades, I have taught Personal Prophesy to men and women around the world from all backgrounds, economic groups, beliefs and cultures. They have been professionals and non-professionals, highly-educated and minimally-educated. In each and every case, it was 100 percent possible to teach these individuals to conduct readings by the Personal Prophesy method accurately.

As you absorb the light of knowledge the cards have to offer, it is amazing how your understanding of the world deepens, and this is reflected in the way you handle situations that confront you and in your dealings with people in general. You begin to anticipate happiness and beautiful new relationships coming your way. Success doesn't feel like a mere pipedream any longer. You can identify potentially traumatic circumstances before they ever become reality and protect yourself from their negative effects or sidestep them altogether. You find that you're able to make choices that steer your life in the right direction, the direction you really want it to go. You begin to fully appreciate the contributions you have to make to the world and the impact your actions clearly have on the lives others are living.

All of this information is readily available to each and every one of us in an ordinary deck of playing cards, every day. It is simply a matter of learning how to harness and properly utilize such amazing information.

This material, which years of study and experience have helped create, is designed to teach you how to be a skilled, insightful, intuitive card reader. By using the techniques described in this book, you will know more than you ever thought was possible about the intricate workings of your own thought patterns, and what it is that makes other people tick. You will learn how to process all of this information and convert it into productive, powerful experience for yourself and those important to you. It requires nothing more than time, concentration, and the drive to see the world with a unique vision that few people ever develop in order to live a happier, more successful life.

I have tried to present the theory and practice involved in reading cards by this method in a conversational, down-to-earth style, designed to help you better understand the principles, theories and their application to everyday life. After all, to *know* something is one thing. To actually harness and use that knowledge properly and effectively is something else. I have tried to discuss each aspect of this fine skill simply and in detail as if I were right beside you, teaching you personally, anticipating the many questions you would have as you were learning. I've also offered practical guidance on emotion, choices, and reading cards expertly for others.

Once you have the fundamentals down and you've achieved the level of intuitive perception necessary to light your own way into the future, you won't need a teacher to show you how to follow any longer. You will be on your own, leading yourself and relying on your own skills to guide you on this challenging journey of enlightenment... and you'll be able to build on this personal knowledge once you have acquired it, for the rest of your life.

A Little Card Reading History

Most historians agree that playing cards as we know them were derived from the Tarot deck, which was probably the first deck of European playing cards. Our modern deck of 52 cards is a shortened version of the Tarot's deck of 78 cards.

The four suits are often thought to parallel the four elements of the universe: water, fire, earth and air. When they are shuffled, as in the elemental process of creation, the results are said to be the forming of the future.

There are two distinct methods of reading playing cards: the English method, which uses the entire deck, and the Italian system, which does not use any of the cards under the number seven. Personal Prophesy uses the entire deck, minus the joker.

Many incredible relationships exist between playing cards and the calendar, which many people are unaware of. For instance, there are twelve face or court cards, directly relating to the twelve months of the year and the twelve signs of the zodiac.

The deck has two colors, red and black, to match the two halves of the year (marked by the summer and winter solstices). The four suits in the deck match the four seasons of the year. There are 52 cards in the deck, just as there are 52 weeks in a year. There are 13 cards in each suit, matching the 13 weeks of each season. Even the number of spots adds up to 365, the number of days in a calendar year.

Playing cards can be said to have a correspondence to the Bible:

The Ace	one God in Heaven.
The Two	the Bible's two sections, The Old and the New Testament.
The Three	the Father, the Son, and the Holy Spirit.
The Four	the four Evangelists of the Gospel: Matthew, Mark, Luke and John.
The Five	five wise maidens were ready to go with their lamps trimmed with oil and five foolish maidens were shut out.

The Six	God's creation of the world in six days.
The Seven	the Sabbath.
The Eight	the eight people who were saved after the flood: Noah, his wife, his three sons, and their three wives.
The Nine	the ten lepers that Jesus cleansed; one came back to give thanks and nine did not.
The Ten	the Ten Commandments.
The King	one King of Kings and Lord of Lords in Heaven.
The Queen	the Virgin Mary, who conceived through the Holy Spirit.
The Jack of Spades	Satan, the Dark Force in life.

So a deck of playing cards can represent an almanac, the Bible, and a system for intuitively interpreting Life's greatest mysteries.

You can learn to intuitively read ordinary playing cards accurately – even expertly – if you are willing to focus, practice and be patient with yourself and your own ability to learn. I have yet to meet an individual who couldn't be taught to be an expert practitioner as long as they are willing to learn the material, practice and devote themselves fully to mastering this skill.

This book is designed for those who have never ventured into the realm of expanding intuitive perception before in their lives. It's designed to help each and every individual acquire a powerful insight about the world, themselves, their lives.

It can literally change your life as you proceed on your own personal journey of self-discovery, learning how to utilize choice and change as instruments in the present to make the future better – in other words, improving the future before you've even lived it!

Introduction

Some people would have you believe the information contained in this book is harmful. Harmful because it offers you a seemingly unfair advantage in life... How to manipulate situations and get the most out of them, how to get ahead.

And, to a certain extent, they would be right; that's what Personal Prophesy offers you. All these amazing intuitive insights... and more. But is any of it really harmful? How harmful is it to become the most successful person you know, if that's what you truly want to be? Or to have the sort of marriage you've always dreamed of? Is it 'harmful' to understand yourself so well that you know exactly what it takes to make you truly happy? Or to have a very clear picture of who your friends actually are? And equally, who your enemies are? Of course, it isn't harmful.

But an awful lot of folks honestly believe that the only way to win in life is to play by the rules, which is exactly what they do every single day of their rut-ridden lives. They pride themselves on having gotten ahead by doing it the hard way, working themselves to the bone, always being humble, blaming every problem that comes along on their own rotten luck.

And yet, true success is something they'll spend their lives chasing after with a butterfly net because they never seem to feel all that happy, all that content, or entirely sure they haven't wasted an incredible amount of time on trial and error, just trying to get it right.

You know something? They have wasted way too much time just guessing what the future might have to offer them, when they could have gotten a good look at it in advance, providing themselves with the opportunity to improve the future before they've even lived it!

Sound incredible? I agree, it does. The concept of being able to accurately perceive the future and being able to act on that knowledge in advance goes against everything we've ever been taught about how to live a happier life. But then, this book is going to throw out just about everything you've ever learned about happiness, anyway.

For instance:

- **Being happy hasn't got a thing to do with being lucky.**
  Lucky people go to Atlantic City. Happy people command their own circumstances and live within the parameters of their own wishes and desires. They literally *make* happiness happen.

- **Every experience, like it or not, is a product of "choice" in one form or another.**
  If you find yourself benefiting from being "in the right place at the right time" it's essentially because *you* put yourself there. *You* made the most productive decisions, which led you to that point in time. On the flip side, if you find yourself suffering calamity after calamity, chances are that you've become the victim of your own faulty decision-making, or you are doing nothing, allowing the choices of others to lead and control your life. If this sounds like you, your life is about to change dramatically for the better. Count on it!

- **No matter how hard we might try to resist it, the fact is, life is nothing but change.**
  We are always changing, always becoming – nothing ever remains the same. Not marriages, friendships, careers, lifestyles. Permanence is only an illusion, something we have created for ourselves in order to feel a sense of security and continuity within the framework of our own day-to-day living. Once you learn how to harness

and productively put to use the powerful energy that is change, it becomes your own creative force for happiness, success, and even personal survival.

Take a good, hard look at where you are in your life. Obviously, things could be better. You are, after all, reading this book, searching for some good, solid answers. Ask yourself what it is you're really yearning for: True love? A prosperous career? Just a good feeling that you're living your life to the fullest?

What if I told you that not only can you have these things, but they're easier to attain than you think? What if I told you that by opening yourself up to what you've always assumed was impossible – consciously living your life in a far more productive, successful and happier manner – you can actually make the items on your life's Wish List very real probabilities, simply by learning the techniques designed to help you get what you want out of life?

All right, it's not quite as easy as that. It will take some work. In some instances, quite a bit of work, but it's all mental effort, and only a little of that effort will go a tremendously long way, as you are about to discover. Immediately after employing just a few of the techniques in this book, you'll begin to look at your life in a whole new way. It's going to feel different to be alive, in control, in charge of yourself and your life's experiences for what may very well be the first time in your life.

In order to make an intuitive experience rewarding in terms of the happiness we want for ourselves as we strive to get what we want out of life, we have to face some enormous misconceptions about our lives that we unconsciously perpetuate as we propel ourselves toward the future. For instance:

- **You were supposed to be happy and successful by now**
  Sound familiar? I'll bet you hear a nagging, little voice in your head harping on about how unhappy and unsuccessful you are nearly every waking moment. Well, you aren't going to listen to that voice anymore. From now on, that voice will be silenced forever. The only voice you'll want to give the time of day to is the

one that speaks from inside your heart, encouraging you to pursue your goals and actively seek the success and happiness you have a right to claim for yourself.

Remember: "To dream is to believe. Once you *believe all things are possible!*" And, *if you can see it, you can be it!*" So go ahead. Dream those dreams. Embrace every last one of those seemingly impossible dreams and let that voice in your heart joyously proclaim *I can*! Dreams are wishes our hearts make, so put aside that belief that dreams don't come true.

As you will soon discover through your study of the Personal Prophesy material, those dreams are a lot closer to becoming reality than you ever thought possible.

- **You should have found your 'one true path' in Life by now**
The fact is, life is a gigantic sea of opportunity. There are more potential paths out there for us to take than we are ever even aware of. The trouble is, until we have developed our intuitive abilities and can see beyond the immediate, we can seldom recognize the right path to take.

  Potential abundance from the Universe escapes us constantly when we have no awareness of what the future holds. But learning how to manipulate the future to steer ourselves toward true happiness, success, fulfillment – whichever happens to top your own personal Wish List – becomes easy, once you have the proper perception to do so.

- **No matter what you do, life will never change**
If you have fallen victim to this ill-gotten belief, which speaks of nothing but the acceptance of an unfulfilled existence, take heart. So has three-quarters of the human race. Why do you think there is so much despair and so little joy in the world? Why else would so many surrender themselves to hopelessness and negativity? It isn't that life never changes, it's that we forget we are the ones holding the power to make it change. Life doesn't change while we sit and wait. We have to open the doors and invite it in.

Personal Prophesy will make you realize that with every morning that dawns, we are the best that mankind can be at that precise moment. With every morning, comes not the same dawn, but a new – a new moment, a new beginning. What we make of it, how we choose to make life better, is entirely up to each of us.

Intuitive Perception as a Tool

What does all of this have to do with perceiving the future through a deck of playing cards? Basically, everything. Finding your life in those cards is an experience in discovery in terms of who you are and where you are in the great big picture called "Life". What you perceive from the cards will be affected by your own personal value system. For instance, if you believe nothing is possible, the cards will reflect that, for your life, nothing is possible. If you are open to change and believe that reality can be shaped and chosen at will, the cards will reflect that, too.

The cards themselves are nothing more than a focal point for you to intuitively perceive what the future holds as potential reality, but the *prophesy* itself is, essentially, what you choose to make of it.

Try as we might, most of us are simply not good navigators when it comes to steering our lives. We tend to thrust ourselves forward without any kind of well-plotted strategy in place, making countless nonsensical choices about our lives in the process.

We recklessly enter ill-fated relationships; take on dead-end jobs, suffer an empty, frustrating existence while never grasping the creative richness of each new day. And we constantly find ourselves haphazardly adjusting to the choices of those around us. Especially those who play important roles in our personal and professional lives: supervisors and co-workers, our relatives, partners and children.

Too often, we put ourselves at the mercy of the needs and desires of those who play these roles in our lives, completely unaware of our own personal power to become the benefactors of the choices we make for ourselves from one day to the next. Instead, we allow the choices of others to dominate our lives. We feel helpless, often victimized, forced to react to the choices of others – choices which dramatically affect our own lives in the process.

Personal Empowerment

Because your own intuitiveness has guided you into reading this book, you won't have to feel helpless and victimized by the world and those in it any longer. As you learn to do readings for yourself and others, you will experience a sense of genuine empowerment you quite likely have never known before.

You will intuitively *know* whether a relationship is right for you even as it is only beginning; which job to take when you are seeking to advance your career; why you are facing a period of deep conflict and struggle at a particular time in your life and what you can do about it.

As a result of such intuitive knowledge, we are able to see how the choices of others dramatically impacts our lives from day to day, how our own choices hold the true key to personal happiness and fulfillment in life.

Wouldn't it be more accurate to say that such a lack of awareness would be far more harmful? You bet it is. Without it, we are basically unconscious travelers on the road to the future who have absolutely no idea where we are headed or what the journey will bring in the end.

As you progress through the lessons in this course, you won't simply learn how to read cards abstractly. You'll read them with meaning and purpose, learning some amazing things about yourself and those around you as you develop expertise in the Personal Prophesy method.

In the process, your own intuitively-inspired journey of self-discovery will inevitably become your best guide toward higher personal enlightenment.

One of the most amazing aspects attached to creating your own destiny with Personal Prophesy is that you can literally begin at any moment. For instance, *this* moment.

Thanks to the power of this wonderful, incredibly dynamic moment we stand in, we can literally change our lives for the better simply by learning how to use that power and energy to our own best advantage.

As a result, our journeys through life become that much more fulfilling. We can shape our destinies in the process. Personal Prophesy readings will guide you well in terms of your own continuing journey from day to day.

By building an intuitive link using playing cards as the focal point to perceive our own futures, the present becomes the best thing to ever happen to us. It offers us the chance to make changes in the future, in essence, *improving the future before we've even lived it!*

Power of the Present

The present is a very powerful moment, which people don't readily realize. They tend to view the present as motionless, fixed, when really the present is very much like standing in a massive breeze as the future is mightily blustering toward you and the past is just as powerfully rushing away.

When you can imagine your present moment as what you experience while standing in a huge breeze, you realize how crucial change really is to your life.

By intuitively perceiving the future from playing cards and putting that insight to use right now, in the present, we have the ability to control and productively put to use the abundant energy which belongs exclusively to this moment we are individually standing in. As a result, change isn't the horrible thing we've always feared. It's actually our very own creative force for happiness and success.

Once you've experienced what it feels like to be in control, living a happier, more productive life because you are able to enjoy the present to the fullest – the present as *you choose* it to be – you'll never want to feel powerless again. I guarantee it.

Chapter One
Your Journey Begins

What does the word "prophesy" mean to you? If you are like most people, the word brings to mind images of things magical, possibly biblical, but most likely improbable – at least as far as modern society is concerned. This is what I have found to be the biggest misconception there is about developing intuitive perception and getting what you want out of life.

The truth is, we are all capable of experiencing the future through this sense, and there is absolutely nothing mystical about it.

Prophesy is simply a message inspired by intuitive thought. The *message* describes aspects of the future before it unfolds, and we all have the natural ability to perceive this message. If you don't believe in your own natural abilities, in your intuitive perception, you might as well live your life in the dark with the blankets pulled up over your head.

The word "prophesy," from here on is only intended to mean: the important message about your life as it is interpreted from the cards.

People often jump to the conclusion that intuitive perception is "fortune-telling." The word "fortune" according to Webster's Dictionary, describes the lot which befalls an individual, whether good or bad, as influenced or controlled by chance. That doesn't describe the message you find in the cards – that is simply a message, not something that controls your fate.

Now, you can say that there are people who seem to lead "fortunate" lives, reaping much "good fortune" as they go, and other people whose lives seem a lot less "fortunate" – and these conditions are often attributed to the natural course of luck. But what people so easily dismiss as "luck" is really nothing more than the end result of the choices they have made.

I have seen people choose love affairs and marriages that are losing propositions, but even if the cards point this out to them, they are led by their conviction to make the unworkable work. People feel trapped in low-paid careers, but choose not to pursue any of the options the cards indicate are open to them, so the dissatisfying situation continues.

Then, there are those people who are so fixated on disaster that they are petrified to make any changes, spending their entire lifetime feeling helpless and victimized. These are truly unhappy people. If you think you are like them, rest assured you are not going to be like them for very much longer.

The bottom line is that all of these people I've described find a compelling sense of security by wallowing in the bleakness of their own poor "luck", and miss the important message of the cards. By doing so, they freely allow the choices of other people to dominate and control their lives.

The Voluntary Shaping of Personal Destiny

Forget about luck, or the "gods" smiling benevolently down upon you. You are going to learn to rely on something far more powerful: Yourself.

Once you accept the message of the cards as the "interpretation of inspiration", which is probably the best definition I have found for the word "prophesy" yet, you will discover this inspiration characterizes a revelation about your life and becomes the stimulus for the most powerful, creative action and thought.

Those who learn to look at Life this way are able to utilize effective decision-making in every facet of their lives and accomplish what the uninformed would call the impossible: The voluntary shaping of personal destiny.

This is something we all do naturally, if not haphazardly, every single day of our lives, simply by exercising our own individual free will. Except those who achieve a unique perception about the future – as you will yourself, very soon – are able to be the benefactors of choice, rather than its victims.

The Voluntary Shaping of Personal Destiny. Sound incredible? I agree it does. That statement contradicts just about everything we've ever been taught about the future since the day we were born. How many times have we all been told that nobody knows what tomorrow will bring? That we should wait and see what happens? What we don't know can't hurt us?

In order to voluntarily shape personal destiny, we have to stop fearing the knowledge of what the future holds and believing that this information is inaccessible to us. In reality, it's right at our fingertips and can be used, every day, to our benefit. We have to stop thinking in terms of "good and bad", hinging all of our hopes and dreams on a "lucky" tomorrow. The time has come to start living happily in the here and now.

By building an intuitive link with your own life and using cards as a focal point to perceive your future, the present can be the best thing that's ever happened to you. Consider, the present provides us with the opportunity to make changes in the future for the better before it even happens. That's pretty powerful stuff we're talking here. And we are all capable of accomplishing this feat.

Before you can take that big step toward a better future, you've got to do one very important thing right now: Make up your mind, once and for all, that you not only *want* to take charge but you *will* take charge of this wondrous, magical thing you call 'your life.' Once you do that, you are ready to start over, *right this very minute.*

If you think about it, all the future really amounts to – no matter how we try to shroud it in mystery – is every moment that comes after *right now.* The past, no matter how we dwell on it and allow it to hold us as emotional, spiritual prisoners, is every moment that came before *right now*. You can't change it, and you can't relive it. It's gone, it's the past.

What does that leave you with? You've got it – the present. That wonderful moment you're standing in *right now*, destined to take on a whole new meaning for you, and in the process, give you power that you wouldn't believe!

The Power of Choice

Once you've learned to control and productively put to use that powerful energy which belongs entirely to the present (and you will), you'll undoubtedly realize that change is not the threat you always thought it to be at all. It's actually your own creative force to wield and utilize as an effective tool toward achieving happiness, success, and genuine love – the future you've always wanted.

How, you ask, can something like that happen? Simply put, because *you* are going to make it happen. As you are about to discover, what you choose for yourself – including all those tiny, seemingly inconsequential choices that you make from day to day – have just as much impact on the events in your life as the major ones do.

Let's take a closer look at this important element, choice. Most people look at their lives as a hodge-podge of good and bad experiences they react to, rather than individually creating for themselves.

Making new friends, getting a better job, an unexpected reunion with a long lost lover – these experiences tend to be considered events created out of or being in the "right place at the right time". Negative experiences are usually blamed on "bad" luck, "bad" breaks, and in general, other people.

Once you start looking at your life as being directed by choice rather than the random effect of things that just "happen", you realize life is nothing but a sequence of choices, large and small, effective and ineffective, causing us to experience certain events and not others.

For instance, let's suppose for a moment that you are romantically involved with someone you originally met through friends. The circumstances for meeting this person aren't all that unusual – let's say you met at a birthday party for one of these mutual friends. Would your decision to attend this party be the only important choice you needed to make in order for you to meet this new love? Or could it actually have been one in a whole series of decisions? Consider: before accepting the invitation to that party, what had to happen? Firstly, you had to be on friendly terms to receive the invitation at all. Therefore, you made the choice to begin and continue a relationship with these people. (And don't forget, they were making equivalent decisions about you!)

Now, in order for that to happen, you had to put yourself in the position to make the acquaintance of at least one of these individuals and. Of course, it could have been one of a hundred different reasons that brought you together, from working at the same company to sharing a cab ride during a snowstorm. Does it matter? The possibilities are virtually endless as to what might have occurred had you chosen differently, but one thing is for certain: You would have presented yourself with a whole new set of events logically leading to a whole new set of experiences!

Let's say that you met one of these people through work – a job you had to make the decision to take, long before you had the opportunity to accept a party invitation. Did you really want that job when it was offered to you? Maybe you had your choice of two different jobs at the time, but you chose this particular one because your own "gut instinct" (intuitive perception) urged you.

Perhaps you made the decision to leave your last position because you were offered this job, a better job. Or maybe you had chosen to get a divorce after years of homemaking, and you felt you needed to re-enter the work force, "unexpectedly" stumbling onto this job while walking down the street. (Not such an "unexpected" event had you known how to intuitively read your own cards!)

At any point during this natural sequence of choices you could have chosen otherwise and naturally altered your own future. But by making the decisions you did, you became involved in an important relationship, which may or may not culminate in marriage, depending on your choice.

Now imagine that you are standing in an employment line with several other people. An executive from a national corporation has been authorized to give good paying jobs to the first ten qualified people waiting in line for employment. Let us assume that the nine people in front of you each hold the necessary qualifications.

With the sequence of choices that got you there and standing in that line at precisely that moment running from A to Z, A was probably your decision to seek a job and Y, your decision to visit the employment office that very morning. Z, of course, has yet to be determined, whether you will choose one of those ten positions.

But suppose some, or even one, of your choices along the way had been altered just a little bit. There are the obvious ones, of course: You chose not to go to the employment office until later that day, you were interviewing for another job across town.

Let's make it a relatively minor alteration. Your car wouldn't start. Rather than stay home, you chose to take the bus – the trouble is it arrived thirty minutes late and the ten good paying jobs had already been distributed by the time you got there. Or suppose your car had started, but on the way into the employment office, you chose to stop and chat with an old friend or use the restroom, causing you to miss the elevator you were trying to catch, finding yourself taking the eleventh place in line. What happens? Obviously, you lose the opportunity with the national corporation and probably blame your own rotten luck for it.

But (and I realize at this point, this "but" is a large one and somewhat difficult to accept) what if you already knew this was not going to be the right job opportunity for you? What if you knew you could have had that job, but you would have missed a better opportunity and wound up stuck in another dead-end job because of one hasty, ill-planned decision on your part?

Could this information be useful to you? Could this information and your use of it help to make the difference between controlling your choices and having them control you?

This is what Personal Prophesy is all about: The ability to control the choices you make and the changes that result by perceiving the future in advance; in essence, providing yourself with the power to alter your future for the better before you've even lived it.

Once you have experienced what it feels like to be in control, living a happier, more productive life because you are able to enjoy the present to the fullest – the present as you choose for it to be – you will never want to spend another day feeling powerless again.

In one way or another, we all cling to our own personal illusions of permanence, allowing ourselves to feel comfortable with a false sense of security about a future we know nothing about. We tell ourselves "wishing will make it so", we are willing to go to all sorts of lengths to restrict ourselves, to resist the dramatic effects of change. By learning to live life more intuitively, the future actually becomes a moment in time that is of our own creation, enabling us to overcome our fears in order to live happily in that new moment.

The Power of the Present

Your journey begins right here, right this moment – this beautiful, wonderful, incredibly powerful moment you are standing in ... experiencing the present in a way which is uniquely your own.

In this book, we will explore all sorts of delightful, inspiring, thought-provoking possibilities. You will learn the meanings of each individual card. You will learn the Personal Prophesy layout, and how to "feel" the cards in a reading, how to read them for yourself.

Let your journey of self-discovery begin slowly, comfortably. Simply say to yourself right now that this is something you can learn. I have done it and others no more special than I am continue to learn to do it every single day.

Intuitive card reading is about as complicated as, say, learning a new language. In fact, Personal Prophesy is very much like a language... the language of the intuitive mind. Most of the people I meet are convinced we are not capable of understanding intuitive thought this well. I disagree.

By teaching you this skill, I will be taking you places in your mind that you probably have never been before. You will feel as if you are traveling into a wonderland you thought only existed in dreams.

Imagine your mind is a house you have been living in all your life, but you never ventured up into the attic or, say, that one room down the hall to which the door has always been closed. Not locked, mind you, just closed.

We will enter that attic or that one room down the hall and when we get there, you won't find anything the least bit strange or sinister at all. You will be absolutely amazed at what you will find...behind that door lies the ability to foresee the future – an incredibly wonderful place to go.

I'll warn you now, your life is going to undergo change as a result of this information, but it is a very positive change. You will realize there isn't a single dilemma in your life that you can't effectively cope with to some degree.

The cards will show you how to *manage* situations more successfully, and when to anticipate problems. Those of you in happy marriages will be able to "key in" on your marriages in the cards and know what to do to keep them happy.

Those who are seeking solid, fulfilling relationships will undoubtedly find them with the guidance of the cards. All of you who have careers will benefit unbelievably, as you learn to use the cards to help you realize your true capacity for success.

You will learn what powerful instruments Choice and Change are and how the sequence of events in your life led you to this moment in the present.

When you have foresight about the future, decision-making, this "choosing" becomes a serious instrument you can actually use to your benefit. You will have knowledge about the outcome of your choices in ways, right now, that may seem unimaginable.

Bear in mind that your morals, attitudes, beliefs will be reflected in the cards when you lay them down for readings. If you are a closed-minded person, narrow or negative in your thinking, your cards are going to reflect that. If you feel doomed to failure, the cards will reflect that too.

If, however, you keep yourself open to opportunity and see life as an immense sea of possibility, your cards will reflect such expansiveness also. In the Personal Prophesy learning process, you will learn a tremendous amount about yourself as well.

A Mini Lesson in Imagery

As we begin the journey you are taking toward living a more insightful, success-filled life, try to imagine your own untapped intuitive perception as something as easy to comprehend as images on a television screen. The people and objects that we watch so intently in the foreground, where most of the action seems to take place, symbolize us... our lives... the events that occur in the present.

When most people watch TV, they tend to be completely caught up in what is happening in the foreground... in other words, "the Present." Most don't pay any attention at all to what there is to see in the background, and yet if they did, they would find a literal universe of information just waiting to be utilized.

The "background" on that TV screen offers all sorts of important information about the environment – the moment – which we rarely even look at. There's atmosphere, activity, even considerable drama taking place that we usually miss in our fascination with the foreground...again, the Present. Think how fulfilling our TV viewing would be if we did pay attention to all those details. It would never be the same for us again.

Visualize your life, right now, as that TV screen. Every image you see on that screen has a reason for being there. Every movement you observe has a purpose for taking place. What's in the foreground? Take a good, hard look at it. The background? Take a good hard look at that too. How much of what you see did you consciously put there? How much would you like to make disappear? You decide. You have the right to decide. That TV screen is projecting a life that belongs to no one but you.

This is what Personal Prophesy is all about: learning to look at your life from this perspective and when you do, the events that occur within the framework of that TV screen don't seem so completely driven by "luck" or "coincidence" anymore. Intuitively speaking, what you interpret from the details in the background of that screen gives meaning to the Present and makes the foreground the richly significant experience that it is.

By personally accepting the message of the cards as the "interpretation of inspiration", which is probably the best definition I have found for the word prophesy, you will find that it characterizes a revelation about your life and becomes the stimulus for the most powerful, creative action and thought.

Those who learn how to use this message are able to utilize effective decision-making in practically every facet of their lives, accomplishing what the uninformed would probably call the impossible: "the voluntary shaping of personal destiny."

This is, of course, something we do every single day, simply by exercising our own individual free will. But those who achieve this unique perception about the future are able to become the benefactors of choice, rather than its' victims.

Building an intuitive link using playing cards as the focal point to perceive your own future, the present becomes the best thing to ever happen to you, in that it gives us the chance to make changes in our future for the better before we've even lived it.

The present is, in fact, a very powerful moment, which people don't often realize. They tend to view the present as motionless, fixed, when really the present is actually very much like standing in a wind tunnel with the future rushing toward you as the past is blustering away. When you can imagine your "present moment" as what you experience in that wind tunnel, you will realize how crucial change really is to your life.

By intuitively perceiving the future in playing cards, you can learn to control and productively put to use that energy that belongs to the present, you find that change is not the horrible thing you've always feared. It becomes your own creative force for happiness, success, love – the future we all want so much to enjoy.

Most people tend to see their lives as a mixture of good and bad experiences they react to, rather than create for themselves.

When you start to look at your life as being directed by choice rather than the random effect of things that just "happen" to you, you begin to understand that life is nothing but a sequence of choices, large and small, effective and ineffective, causing us to experience certain events and not others.

Having prior knowledge of events like this is very useful information. This information and the way a person uses it can mean the difference between controlling your choices and having them control you. This is the essence of Personal Prophesy: Acquiring the ability to control the choices you make and the changes that result by perceiving the future in advance; providing yourself with the power to alter your future for the better before you've even lived it.

Once you've experienced what it feels like to be in control, living a happier, more productive life because you are able to enjoy the present to the fullest – the present as you choose for it to be – you'll never want to feel powerless again.

The future begins right here... let's get started on making it happen, shall we?

Chapter Two
Expanding Intuitive Perception

Congratulations on turning the page and opening yourself up to an entirely new way of life.

If you've never picked up a deck of ordinary playing cards and found your life waiting to be interpreted from them, are you in for a wonderful surprise. Not only can you find all sorts of information about your past, present and future in those 52 cards – you can put that insight to work for yourself in ways you probably don't think are even possible.

The amazing part about learning this skill is that it is just that: – a skill. Perceiving your life from a deck of ordinary playing cards is *not* an impossible feat. I do it and others no more "psychic" or "spiritual" than I am do it constantly. All we possess is an acquired intuitive perception about ourselves and the lives we're living. Nothing more.

How did we acquire this unique perception that makes it possible for us to find our lives in an ordinary deck of cards? We worked and studied to develop it, pure and simple. As a result, we've been able to achieve a viewpoint about life in general that is more *intuitive* than that of the average person on the street. In case you didn't know, this happens to be the big secret behind the thriving business of providing psychic readings to the public in the first place.

Here's why: Intuitive perception is an expandable sense, common to everyone. We are all capable of developing this perception and exercising it, skillfully and with purpose, even though few people ever do.

It's probably one of the best-kept secrets there is. In certain circles – especially those that are commercially motivated – intuitive perception is a tremendously big secret. We're talking about people who are perceptual masters of this sense and the ability to make money from such an ability, and they know it, having cashed in on it in a huge way by touting themselves as "gifted". Why would they ever want to share this secret with the rest of the world, forcing them to stop making all that money?

That's the last thing they would ever want to do. It's also the reason why professional card readers aren't apt to lose any sleep over the rest of us trying to learn how to read cards from books written on the subject. They rest on their "psychic" laurels, convinced that few of us will ever be able to do it right.

As you can imagine, this inability on the part of the public to accurately conduct a reading adds tremendously to the mystique – not to mention the money-making potential – which has always surrounded the skill of card reading. While books show us *how* to do it, in painstaking meticulous detail, these books inevitably fail to teach us what we really need to know:

The big secret is that it is intuitive perception, which ultimately makes a good, accurate reading possible. Without that perception, how can you ever know what you "see" in those cards.

This book is intended to put an end to all that "only a gifted reader can achieve an accurate reading with cards" profit-generating mystery, forever.

Your Own Personal Symbolism

It is a generally accepted among those who have expertise in reading cards that no two people interpret the cards in quite the same fashion. I agree with this theory 100 percent. Interpretation of the symbolism is as individual as a signature.

Perception is a uniquely personal process. No two human beings see things alike, feel emotions in the same way, or share identical life experiences to support their own personal value systems. Your own intuitive perception will reflect this individuality.

So how is it that I can presume to teach prophesy with cards when it is obviously something so personal? Simple. And this is the part I've never found in any other book on card reading, anywhere – what I consider to be the very key to the whole mystery: The symbolism is something *you* must develop for yourself. It comes from within you to be put to use by you and only you, ultimately producing the most accurate readings possible. All I can do is help you get there, step by step.

Let's begin with a little *Imagery*.

Suppose that I am there with you. Really try to put some effort into this: Imagine what I look like, how my voice sounds. Feel how close I am to you. Really *see* me. I am no longer merely words on the page, but a thinking, breathing, feeling human being at your side.

What you will learn to find in an ordinary deck of cards is going to seem as real to your mind's eye as I do right now in this mental image you've just created of me.

Imagine that I am handing you a ring of keys. There are 52 keys on this ring, just as there are 52 cards in the deck – but don't let this number overwhelm you. In time, you will feel just as comfortable with the keys on this ring as you do the ones you carry in your pocket every day.

I know which doors those 52 keys belong to. These doors are the literal meanings of each of the cards. What you will find behind those doors is your own *interpretation* – that all-important symbolism I mentioned to you earlier. From my own perspective of having turned the locks with these keys and opened every one of those doors myself, I am familiar with what those keys represent. I already know that all the keys on that ring are uniquely individual. To you, it's probably just a ring of keys that basically look the same, for now. Once you have experienced what is behind each of the special doors I am about to lead you through, you will share that perspective of recognition and familiarity. I guarantee, with time and practice, it can be done.

We are going to go through the your ring of keys – the deck of cards – card by card. It's an ordinary deck of playing cards, remember. These cards do not have special powers. It is not a magic card trick. The cards simply provide you with a message through the expansion of your intuitive perception.

Bringing Symbolism to Life

Bear in mind that I am giving you the literal meanings of the cards, as I know them. The symbolism you will experience with the right effort and concentration is something you can't be told, you have to find it for yourself. Since this is an extremely complex step and the most important in terms of future success in getting what you want from your life, I strongly recommend that as I lead you, you find each card in your own deck and you study it carefully. Look at each card slowly and carefully, as if you were committing that card to memory. As you do this, you will begin to create your own intuitive link with that card, which is vital for proper reading ability.

As you look into each card and you build that link, which I'll tell you right now, is a very slow and intense process that won't happen overnight, you will find yourself beginning to experience a unique feeling or perception about that card. It originates from the symbolism you gained when you opened its door with the right key.

When you become aware of this unique feeling and you find you experience it every time you see that card, you will be well on your way to developing the necessary sensitivity that supports your intuitive link. This sensitivity is vital to your ability to interpret the prophesy within the cards accurately, skillfully, and with ease.

The mistake an enthusiastic student can make at this point is in concentrating on too many cards too soon. Take your time. Three or four a day is plenty for you to gain steady progress. If you find you have trouble building that crucial link with your cards, take two or three with you in your pocket, and leave them under your pillow at night. Study them before going to sleep and again in the morning. You'll be amazed how quickly your intuitive perception can develop.

Don't give up. By concentrating and consistently working at it, the necessary perception will eventually come to you as naturally as saying your own name. It *will* come. It takes time. Be prepared to invest the time. Once accomplished, the rest of your journey to powerful self-discovery will belong to no one but you.

Learning About Yourself and Others

When you have foresight about the future, decision-making, this choosing becomes a serious instrument you can use to your benefit. You will have knowledge about the outcome of your choices in ways that may seem unimaginable. You'll also come to understand the true essence of the hearts of those around you, what makes them tick and how in tune they really are with their own emotions.

You won't be fooled by a misguided sense of trust any longer when it comes to others. Liars and cheats? You'll be able to identify them clearly in your readings. Fair weather friends will be obvious to you. Whether a marriage will last or a job will flourish... It's all waiting to be perceived in a deck of playing cards.

You don't have to be gifted to do these things. Intuitively reading cards is a skill like any other, typing, solving math problems, sewing, carpentry... it's just a somewhat unusual one, in that so few people ever take the time to expand their own intuitive sense in order to perceive the future. This sense, in terms of Personal Prophesy, is like a piece of elastic. It has the ability to stretch... and stretch.. .and stretch. I am still expanding my own sense over 20 years later.

Bear in mind that your own morals, attitudes, beliefs will be reflected in the cards when you lay them down for readings. If you are a closed-minded person, narrow or negative in your thinking, the cards are going to reflect that. If you feel doomed to failure, the cards will reflect that.

If, on the other hand, you keep yourself open to opportunity and see life as an immense sea of possibility, your cards will reflect such expansiveness. In the process of learning Personal Prophesy you will learn a tremendous amount about yourself as well. Your perception of life and the future as you take this course will reflect your own moral, emotional and spiritual values. The "feelings" you give to the cards, individually and collectively, will belong to no one but you.

A Mini Lesson

If you are a complete newcomer to the skill of reading playing cards, you may question your own ability to intuitively read playing cards successfully. Equally, if all you know is what you've learned from reading Tarot cards, the following is a Personal Prophesy mini lesson to help acquaint you with this method.

Remember: Your own perception of life and the Past, Present and Future as you take this course will reflect your own moral, emotional and spiritual values. The emotional feelings you attach to the cards, individually and collectively, will ultimately belong to no one but you.

To illustrate this point, imagine that I am now handing you a color sample as I tell you, "This is the color green."

Each of you will see that green-ness in your own distinct way. Some of you will instantly love the color and feel inexplicably drawn to it. On a deep inner level, you've lived all your life well acquainted with the emotional connotations you attach to that shade of green, so you understand that green-ness very well within the context of your own lives.

Perhaps it symbolizes remembrances of lovely times that you characterize as happy green moments celebrated in your life. Perhaps it signifies true simplicity, harmony and peace, a blanket of comfort and security characterized by that shade of green. You may not even be able to consciously understand why you find the color so easy to positively interpret emotionally. It simply is green.

Others, however, will feel compelled to dislike that particular shade of green. Perhaps the color represents a room where you have spent unhappy times. It may emotionally resurrect the tragic memory or accident.

Such early experiences impact our perceptions of things later in life. Whether you react positively or negatively to a simple shade of the color green is a good example of how you will come to feel about most of the cards in the deck as you learn them and later, do readings with them.

Ultimately, you will also bring the same *essence of your own inner being* to your perceptions whenever you view an aspect of the Past, Present and Future in your readings.

Achieving Accurate Symbolism in Readings

We have now ventured into territory that never fails to separate the amateurs from the pros every time when it comes to card reading. In a word: Interpretation.

Those who have enough experience reading cards will wholeheartedly agree that no two readers interpret the cards in quite the same way. The interpretation of each card is as individual as a signature. Perception will always be a very personal and individual process where interpretation of the cards is concerned.

When you consider that people don't view the world through the same eyes or experience emotions in the same manner, nor do they share identical memories or life experiences supporting personal value systems, how could their perceptions when they intuitively read cards ever be the same? They couldn't be.

Your own interpretations of the cards will reflect this same kind of individuality 100 percent of the time.

To illustrate what I mean by the feelings you will give to the cards, let's learn one right now: the Four of Hearts. I can tell you that the Four of Hearts means jealousy and describe it in detail, but to properly read the cards you need to know how each of them "feels". Remember back to a time in your life when you lost someone you loved to someone else. Really "feel" that moment and recall the experience from your past, that horrible, gnawing, ugly feeling. It's a feeling we never forget.

If you've never lost a lover in such a way, recall a job or an award you yearned for which was ultimately given to someone else. Go as far back in your past as you need to in order to find a moment in your life to revive that gnawing, relentless feeling. Once you do, what you are actually experiencing about this card is, in fact, the essence of the Four of Hearts.

The teaching material contained in this book will help you learn to "feel" each of the cards in the deck in this manner. Every card in one fashion or another, as you will soon learn, possesses its own distinctive *feeling* or meaningful *symbolism*. My mission is to take you through the cards and the Personal Prophesy philosophy, step by step, providing you with the seeds of knowledge; the rich, life-filled garden of insight you grow as a result will belong entirely to you. As you read and learn, you will find your garden flourishing.

Experiencing Emotion Intuitively

Some people just are not in touch with the intuitive side of their minds. Some are fearful of experiencing emotion, particularly those more painful or negative emotions. Some are afraid to be happy, to know what happiness feels like, and tend to go through life with blinkers on emotionally.

I'll warn you right now: you will intuitively "see" things in the cards that you won't like. The cards are expert at giving us messages we may not want to receive. A friend you trust may not be perceived as deserving of such loyalty. A partner might love you less than you think. Your boss may be making plans to replace you by the end of the year. Occasionally, you will perceive such startling revelations as impending *Death*.

Intuitively speaking, Death is only in the rarest of cases considered to be a physical death when you perceive this message in a reading. Often, such perception is intended to prepare us of unavoidable situations where physical death has the potential for becoming reality. You will learn to use these cards to caution people. To be especially careful yourself until the warning passes from the cards.

Most times you will see Death in the cards as a far more realistic "death of circumstances", where one set of circumstances has to "die" before another can be "born". For instance, when someone stops loving you, you will experience the "death" of his or her love. One door closing in life as another opens... the end of one phase and the beginning of another.

When you perceive personal tragedies approaching for others in your cards, all you can ever do is attempt to steer the recipient of your reading to some level of deeper understanding.

It can be an extremely huge burden to carry from the point of view of *perceiver of tragedy*. We must always remember that we are never anywhere close to assuming the position and power of the Higher Power, God, the Life Source, however you personally conceive the power of the Universe to be spiritually.

Consider, I wouldn't be terribly successful today if I had spent the past two decades conducting readings for the public declaring, "Your husband is a real jerk, you'd better go home and dump him". Such a step from the present to the future is entirely up to the recipient to decide *for him/herself.*

Your job as a practitioner of the Personal Prophesy method is simply to try to help people with relationship problems find workable solutions in order to effectively cope with them; to see the options; to essentially feel hope that there is a positive conclusion.

The mind is, after all, an extremely powerful instrument in and of itself.

Chapter Three
Learning the
Suit of Hearts

Your personal journey of self-discovery in terms of learning Personal Prophesy takes shape with this lesson on the Suit of Hearts and the meanings of the individual cards contained in it.

Please don't take notes as you read this lesson. Allow yourself the opportunity to simply "experience" the meanings of the cards, one by one, as you read about each of them. At the end of this lesson, you will find a summary of these cards, which you will be able to go back and study from in the future.

"Experiencing" or visualizing the cards is the first step toward understanding Personal Prophesy, enabling you to intuitively perceive important messages from the cards for yourself and for others when you conduct a reading. It is suggested that you take the entire suit of Hearts from a deck of playing cards as you read through this lesson, so that you can study each card as they are individually described.

Bear in mind that most of the cards in the deck are highly complex in nature. The meanings are specifically designed for the Beginner's Level to be simple and easily understood.

The first card in the suit of Hearts is

The Two of Hearts – Personal Fulfillment

On the intuitive level, this is a wonderful, wonderful card – perhaps the best card in the whole deck. The literal meaning of this card is

Ambition & Personal Fulfillment, but in order to accurately read this card, you must actually "feel" it.

Imagine yourself right now, standing before an audience and they are all applauding you and your achievement, cheering you on, urging you to reach even greater heights of success. Think about that feeling. You have finally made it. You are what you always dreamed you'd be. This is the essence of the Two of Hearts – it is an extremely powerful card in terms of its prophesy.

Visualize yourself doing that something you've always dreamed of for yourself, whether it's singing or painting, being a lawyer or a parent. What that achievement represents to you is what the Two of Hearts is all about. It represents accomplishment and joy over a realized dream.

This card will help you find the right job when you are job hunting. It will help you find the right marriage partner. The feeling attached to this card lets you know that you are on the right road to success.

The Three of Hearts – Regret

This is a card that literally means Regret and Sorrow, but to actually feel it, imagine that you have just broken something precious that perhaps belongs to a close friend, perhaps a vase or a china cup, something they hold very dear.

See this object as a thing lying in pieces on the floor between you. This card is about feeling sorry about something that is beyond repair – as in a broken relationship – but for now, simply see it as a shattered object which would take considerable effort to repair, and there is much regret and sorrow attached to the shattering of it.

In a future chapter, we will discuss the philosophy called the Evolution of Emotion and discover that feelings evolve into newer, better, more meaningful feelings even after they have been "shattered" as in this visualization. This is a deep subject and not required to be understood as you learn the simple meanings of the cards.

The Four of Hearts – Jealousy

To feel it, imagine a time when you lost someone you loved to another. Or you went to court to fight a case that meant a great deal to you and the opposing party won the case, hands down.

Feel that feeling. It's a gnawing, gut-wrenching, sick feeling focused on wanting what someone else has. You'll find out later that this card also pulls in hatred and revenge in terms of definition, but for now, just think utter and complete jealousy.

The Five of Hearts – Gift

This is a lovely, feel good card. It literally means a gift, a compliment, the giving of something very special to someone else. See it as a bouquet of flowers being handed to you. It feels nice.

If you are allergic to flowers, think of something just as nice: a great big, beautifully-wrapped gift being given to you and in it is something very nice. The meaning of this card is the same whether you are receiving that gift or giving it... just get that good feeling associated with this card.

The Six of Hearts – Promise

This is a truly fantastic card. It is your very own "yellow brick road" card. It means "great promise" or "a bright road" and you should visualize it as a sunny and bright path leading into the future.

It's a card that means a lot when connected to courtship and marriage. It can be an excellent card to intuitively think of in terms of work-related matters as well. This card lets you know that you are traveling in the right direction, that the future holds great potential for personal happiness, that you can feel optimistic about a particular relationship or enterprise. It signifies your own flower-trimmed and sunny "yellow brick road" to the future.

You have learned enough, thus far, to attempt reading your very first spread – three cards laid out in a reading, together. Don't worry about reading format; we will get to that in a later lesson. This exercise is to simply help build your confidence that you can learn to read cards by this method.

You've learned three of the most wonderful cards so far. This will be your first experience at actually reading them.

Visualize the Two of Hearts: that feeling of accomplishment. Combine that feeling with the Five of Hearts: a lovely gift. Now, add to what you are feeling, the Six of Hearts: a bright, beautiful road ahead.

These three cards together are considered to be connected to each other and would comprise a reading, a "spread" as you will learn later on. If you can experience those three cards as a combined feeling, these cards together in a reading would indicate abundant personal success and many rewards and gifts coming on the path you are currently taking into the future.

If you can't yet feel it, don't worry. That feeling of having accurately experienced the cards and intuitively understanding their message for you will come. It takes time and practice, but it will come.

Continuing on...

The Seven of Hearts – Friendship

This is another excellent card in terms of it's prophesy. It literally means genuine friendship. Recall a time when you've had a really true friend in your life. Not a sort of friend or a sometimes friend, a really true friend. Someone who platonically loved you, no matter what. Someone who suffered your sorrows and celebrated your joys as if they were their own, a true-to-the-end, honest-to-goodness friend.

This card will let you know, beyond a shadow of a doubt, who your friends really are. The Seven of Hearts does not show up in readings nearly as often as you might expect it to. True, honest friends are rare and extremely hard to come by. Most, as you will discover as you advance in the study of Personal Prophesy, fall into the category of being very good friends who enjoy the good times with you. But the instant conflict is encountered in those friendships, they become birds in flight, immediately fleeing the relationship they have shared with you.

You are going to learn some startling things about your life and the people in it when you start reading these cards for yourself. You will see who really is your friend, who really loves you, and who is less then true.

Ignorance may be bliss, but your cards are going to put reality in your face, every time. You will learn to be cautious about who you trust from now on.

This card, Friendship, the Seven of Hearts is actually the best foundation for marriage, but so few tend to see it that way. Most base a lifetime on passion and excitement, which is not the most stable stuff for permanency.

The Eight of Hearts – Celebration

This is a fun card. It literally means party or celebration. Imagine a big celebration... everybody's happy and smiling. This card lets you know in readings that good times are approaching. You will enjoy yourself and the occasion is coming in the near future.

The Eight of Hearts is a card imparting a good feeling, especially welcome when you find yourself reading cards that are basically negative in nature. With a celebration on the horizon, things are obviously not that bad.

The Nine of Hearts – The Wish card

This is the most important card in the deck. It essentially means nothing by itself. The Nine of Hearts is your "wish card". When you read the cards to receive an answer to a personal question or you are conducting a reading for someone else, this is the card you are looking for in these readings. This card tells you the outcome of the question you ask.

It is the official Wish Card. It is telling you that the cards connected to it in the spread are the answer to your question.

You do not always get your wish. Sometimes, the card will tell you quite emphatically, "This is not a good thing to be wishing for". Often you will do a reading for people and see that they are wishing for all the wrong things. Doomed relationships, jobs that will never come though, affairs that will only break their hearts are things you may find. You can share with them the prophesy of the cards, but getting them to heed it is another story entirely.

The Nine of Hearts points to answers. It tells you the outcome of their wish and that wish is generally for knowledge about something. Lots of people will keep wishing but all you can do is tell them what you see as the intuitive answer. That's when you try to steer them away from the Nine of Hearts and get them to look for the potential in the Ten of Hearts.

The Ten of Hearts – True Love

This card is completely centered on true love. Real love. The love that can survive just about anything. When this card appears in a reading connected to a relationship, you can accomplish all together and overcome any obstacle.

It is your moment of beginning again through the bonds of love. This card will tell you in no uncertain terms who loves you and who doesn't. You may be very surprised, when you read the cards, to perceive who really does love you.

When you get to know your own cards well you may recall their message when it comes true. When you meet someone who you have perceived in the cards long before this individual came into your life as truly having the potential to love you, you may feel this urge when you do actually meet to say, "Oh my goodness! You're going to love me!" That's how accurate, how strong and how meaningful the love attached to this card is.

Now, the face cards in the Suit of Hearts are people who are represented in readings by a Heart face card. Face cards always represent people. Please take this segment of the lesson somewhat loosely if you can, so you won't get hung up on the people characteristics.

Those characterized as a Heart face card in readings are perceived to be extremely giving and loving, humanitarian in their views on life, sensitive to the needs of others, true care givers in every sense of the word.

The Jack of Hearts – Young at Heart

This card signifies a man, usually with green eyes and dark blond to auburn hair, who has humanitarian ideals, and who is either young in age or in terms of maturity. The maturity I'm referring to concerns the spirit of the male represented by this card. It doesn't necessarily indicate youth in terms of age, although it will sometimes. Essentially the male represented by the Jack is young at heart and still somewhat inexperienced in the ways of life. The Jack is a man still learning the ropes. Jacks don't have an abundance of wisdom to impart... that's more the King's job.

The King of Hearts – Maturity

He represents a man with green eyes and dark blond to auburn hair who is older in age or very mature in his thought patterns. The King has essentially mastered the things the Jack is still learning. He is perceived as a wise, mature spirit, even though he may be young in his actual years.

The Queen of Hearts – a Woman

She signifies a female figure in the reading you are conducting. The Queen of Hearts represents a caring woman with green eyes and dark blond to auburn hair.

The Ace of Hearts – Home

This is a neutral card. It signifies the Home or those matters regarding to the home.

A Summary of the Suit of Hearts

The following descriptions of the cards are intended to help you generate an image in your own mind of that card's essence. Don't become too locked in on the literal meanings given here... allow yourself to feel the flow of intuitive thought on each.

TWO of HEARTS	Signifies ambition and personal fulfillment. Remember the feeling of an accomplished personal dream, the sense of having made it. Excellent aspects when joined with career and marriage cards.
THREE of HEARTS	Signifies sorrow and regret. The feeling of having broken a friend's precious possession, of realizing you broke it. Apologies perceived in the cards will be joined with this card.
FOUR of HEARTS	Signifies jealousy, resentment, and malice. The feeling of anger mixed with pain when someone takes the person you love away.
FIVE of HEARTS	Signifies a gift or compliment. The feeling of receiving a beautiful bouquet of flowers.
SIX of HEARTS	Signifies great promise. The feeling of a bright and sunny road to the future, like the yellow brick road. It involves personal and professional relationships that develop into marriages or partnerships with tremendous potential for success.
SEVEN of HEARTS	Signifies genuine friendship, pure platonic love. This card will show you who your true friends are, the ones who will be beside you through thick and thin.
EIGHT of HEARTS	Signifies celebration. The feeling of being at a party, having fun, good times.
NINE of HEARTS	Signifies a neutral wish card. This card means nothing by itself. The other cards around it will tell whether your wish will be harmful or helpful to you.
TEN of HEARTS	Signifies true love, unity. The feeling of love that can last through anything and everything. You know that with this person by your side, you can accomplish anything and overcome all obstacles.

JACK of HEARTS	Represents a male, usually with green eyes and dark blond to auburn hair, who is either young in age or young in maturity, but has humanitarian ideals.
QUEEN of HEARTS	Represents a caring woman with green eyes and dark blond to auburn hair.
KING of HEARTS	Represents a man with green eyes and dark blond to auburn hair, who is older in age or older in maturity. Personality Characteristics: Loving, caring, humanitarian, care giving.
ACE of HEARTS	Signifies the home. The other cards surrounding the Ace of Hearts will show you the other influences surrounding the home.

Homework Practice

Homework is designed specifically to help you develop confidence in your own card reading skills. Separate the suit of Hearts from a deck of playing cards. Shuffle the Hearts only. Deal out three cards face up. From what you have just learned, focus on what you "feel" about these three cards and their interaction. There are no right or wrong answers, so let your own intuitive ability be your guide. Repeat this exercise until you are comfortable with the meanings and feelings associated with the suit of Hearts.

Chapter Four
Learning the Suit of Spades

As we continue to learn, card-by-card, the four suits of the deck, keep reminding yourself that it is an ordinary deck of playing cards you are holding in your hands. These cards do not have any special powers. This is not magic or card tricks you're learning. The cards are simply keys which open your intuitive mind so that you can receive the messages they have to offer through your own personal expansion of intuitive perception.

Bear in mind as we progress that I am giving you the literal meanings of the cards as I know them. The *symbolism* you will come to experience, with the right amount of effort and concentration, will be your own once you feel that intuitive link beginning to develop within yourself when you view the cards.

This symbolism is something you can't be taught; you must find that for yourself in the cards. Since this is an extremely complex step and the most important in terms of future success in reading cards by the Personal Prophesy method, I strongly recommend that, as I lead you, you find each card in your own deck and you study it carefully. Look at each card slowly and carefully, as if you were committing that card to memory.

As you look at each card, you will begin to create your own intuitive link with that card, which is absolutely essential for proper reading ability. As you build that link, which is a slow and intense process that won't happen overnight, you'll find yourself beginning to experience an incredibly unique feeling or perception about that card. It originates from the symbolism you gained when you opened the door to that card with the right key.

When you become aware of this unique feeling and you find you experience it every time you see that particular card, you will be well on your way to developing the necessary sensitivity which supports your intuitive link. This sensitivity is vital to your ability to interpret the prophesy within the cards accurately, skillfully, and with ease.

Be prepared to take the time. By concentrating and consistently working at it, the necessary perception will eventually come to you as naturally as saying your own name. It will come. It takes time. Once accomplished, the rest of your journey to discovery belongs to no one but you.

In this lesson, you will study the suit of Spades and the meanings of the individual cards contained in it. In contrast to the suit of Hearts, Spades are, by nature, very heavy cards in terms of their literal meanings. You may find them downright depressing as you learn them.

Personal growth, however, doesn't always occur in a loving, tender, sensitive-to-your-needs atmosphere that the suit of Hearts tends to represent. The deepest part of an individual grows and inner strength develops from experiences of intense sadness, anguish and unexpected change – in other words, experiences characterized by the Suit of Spades.

The first card in this suit is

The Two of Spades – Abrupt Change

To feel the message of "abrupt change" contained in this card, visualize yourself walking forward in a straight line. All of a sudden, you take a decisive turn. The direction isn't what matters most in this mental picture, the fact is, your course has suddenly, abruptly changed. Do you get that feeling of change as you imagine yourself taking that turn? If so, you are getting the message of the Two of Spades.

Often, new partners in dating situations go through abrupt changes in their emotions in this way. The beginning of a new romantic relationship is, after all, quite fragile. It can change just like that.

Married people, or those who are in long-term committed relationships, tend to waver back and forth... the line of change is more of a squiggly line, rather than a right-angle turn in another direction. When these people are contemplating change – which those in shaky marriages tend to do quite frequently – they aren't quite sure what they want to do and, so they don't make the abrupt changes which are represented by this card.

We will get more into the philosophy of Change later on. For now, just remember that the Two of Spades indicates "abrupt change".

The Three of Spades – Running Errands

This is an interesting little card. This card references short trips, running errands, taking care of "trivial matters" – but something surprising is being indicated by this card as occurring rather unexpectedly as you go about those matters we often refer to as "routine business". Make sure you see "movement" attached to this card as you visualize it – it isn't about sitting at a desk. You are moving around. For instance, it could indicate going to the grocery store and running into an old friend you haven't seen in quite some time. Or you take your dog for a walk and run into a long lost love on the way.

It's a very good card. Think of it as taking care of routine matters, with unexpected experiences in the process.

Now, starting with the Four of Spades, we are going to enter varying layers of feeling attached to the suit of Spades.

The Four of Spades – Sickness

This is a sick card, it indicates illness, physically and also that of the spirit. With practice you will learn to intuitively know the difference. It is a card representing depression, negativity, lack of well-being. Think of sitting in the house with a terrible cold looking out on a rainy, dreary afternoon.

To give you an idea how you would read this card, mentally take that Four of Spades and blend it with the feeling of the Four of Hearts: Jealousy. Combined together, they produce a sick, jealous feeling. Feel that feeling. No good will come of those two cards blended that way, except that you'd be thinking you don't want to feel that way for very long.

If you threw a strong Love card on that mix of jealousy and illness, you'd have quite an emotional crisis building there. Or a dangerous situation, depending on the mental stability of the individual involved.

The Five of Spades – Anger

This card represents deep, dark, nasty, seething anger. But anger can be a very positive force at times, propelling us toward productive Change.

In your readings, it will resemble a forest fire. Burning down all the trees, but what grows later from among all that ash can be fuller, healthier, much stronger trees in the end. The fire represented by this card is destructive at the time it occurs; it can even be downright dangerous if not properly controlled. But it clears the way for rebirth and renewal and brings new insights, new growth, and a place for starting fresh, in the end.

The Six of Spades – Caution (or Pregnancy)

This is a somewhat unusual card. Some of the cards will seem rather sketchy at first; not all of the cards are as intense in feeling as "anger."

This card literally has two meanings. With time and practice, you will learn to know the difference in a reading. The most important meaning (although the other can be very important too, as you'll soon see) is that this card indicates caution in your readings. It is a card that warns you..."there may be trouble ahead" or "You aren't getting the full story, so hold yourself in check." See it as a big flashing yellow light. It's definitely a card to pay attention to, when it appears in your readings. It is advising you to hold back, to walk into a situation slowly, to keep your emotions in reserve.

The other meaning attached to the Six of Spades is Pregnancy! This card has predicted more pregnancies than I could ever begin to tell you over the years in readings I've conducted, so it would be a good thing to bear in mind that this card has a dual meaning.

In general, heed the message of the Six of Spades. Most of the time, it will be saying, "Be cautious at this time."

Beginning with the Seven of Spades, we're going to take a journey into degrees of pain.

The Seven of Spades – Loss

This is a card that means Loss. To feel this card, remember back to when we covered the Three of Hearts (regret) in your last lesson and that china cup you suddenly broke which belonged to someone dear to you which could not be repaired. Take that visualization a step further by imagining that cup was the only one of its kind on the planet and it is virtually priceless. Once broken, it's gone forever and you never quite get over its loss.

As in the loss of a parent or a true love, or if your dog ran away and never comes back. Find your own personal point of reference for this card in terms of deep, utter Loss.

Whenever you look back on this incident, the wound still seems to be fresh. It never seems to heal. Closure, in this lifetime, may never be possible. It resembles scar tissue over an incision. Things are never the same and that scar will always be a reminder.

The Eight of Spades – Tears

This card means tears; these are fresh, heart-broken tears of pain, but also cleansing, healthy, healing tears in the end. Shedding tears is very good for the spirit as tears put us in touch with our emotions. Much like rain after the forest fire, they represent the water, which is necessary to promote new growth for the future.

When you see the Eight of Spades connected to someone in the cards who has recklessly turned his or her back on you in anger, this is an indication that this person is moving toward Change emotionally and those tears are guiding them to feel remorse for their actions. Tears represent longing to go back and make things right. While we can never go back, we can certainly move forward and through the cleansing power of tears, make things right in the future.

The Nine of Spades – Grief

This is a deeply intense card, indicating grief, agony, suffering. You might visualize this card as a person sitting in a cold, barren room with their head in their hands, sobbing.

How do the Seven and Nine of Spades differ, you may wonder? Let's say your father dies. You had a warm, loving relationship with your dad. You will always miss him terribly. This feeling would be indicative of the loss described by the Seven of Spades.

But let's say you had a father who, all your life, turned his back on you. Even when you needed him and reached out to him, he never fully acknowledged you with love. Then he dies and you realize you will never have the chance to know that man as a true father Feel that unresolved grief. That is the feeling behind the Nine of Spades.

Some visualize the Nine of Spades as the grief you feel when you lose the person, and the Seven of Spades as representing the loss of the relationship. You will develop your own personal emotional links to these cards and once you do, you will never forget them.

The Ten of Spades – a Journey

This is another neutral card. It simply means a journey, a physical journey in the sense of going away or coming back. Some of the cards don't have emotion attached to them. They are merely cards characterizing movement. This card is one of them. The Ten of Spades will generally involve long distance travel. But distance will become a personally relative term for you as you conduct your own readings.

Now, the people cards associated with the Suit of Spades. Spades people tend to have a rather dark complexion, brown hair, brown eyes. But don't become fixated on the physical characteristics of any of the suits when you read the cards. Allow the people in your life to come through in your readings as whichever face card happens to represent them best.

People who come through in a reading as being represented by a Spades face card are seen as being very analytical and logical by nature. They are driven by their minds, not their hearts. They are not especially emotionally-inclined. Spades people make excellent judges, lawyers, purveyors of justice.

The Queen of Spades – a Woman

This card will always represent a female. She is mentally sharp, and judges situations with her mind rather than her heart.

The Jack of Spades – a Young Man

The Jack of Spades represents a young male in age or mentality, who places logic before emotional concerns and can be judgmental.

The King of Spades – an older, authoritative Man

This card will represent a man in your readings who is older in terms of his age or spirit. He is the lawyer or the judge, fair minded.

The Ace of Spades – Ending

The Ace of Spades is another "neutral" card in the Personal Prophesy method. Be aware that it has two meanings.

When the point (the apex) is upside down, it indicates distance, something occurring in a distant location. It always symbolizes physical miles. In other words, the event or the person involved is at a distance.

When the point (or apex) is upright, this card indicates conclusion, an ending, a death of circumstances. In some instances, very few, it can indicate death. There is a natural progression of life in this method of card reading. In death, there is always a new beginning. You have to help the person you are reading for emotionally make that leap from conclusion to new beginning. As one door closes, another opens.

Too many people want to cling to yesterday and refuse to accept that life is all about new beginnings. Change is frightening to many people. They don't realize that Change is the only constant in life.

As you learn Personal Prophesy, you will discover that the death of present circumstances represented by the Ace of Spades is a beautiful, open door in which you can walk to a happier, more fulfilling tomorrow.

Here are simple descriptions for the Suit of Spades. These descriptions are not to be taken as literal meanings, they are intended to help you generate an image in your own mind of that card's essence. Allow yourself to feel the flow of intuitive thought on each.

Summary of The Suit of Spades

Two of Spades	Signifies change. It's the feeling of walking in one direction then suddenly you take a step in another direction and continue on from there. This card deals with a definite change of course.
Three of Spades	Signifies routine matters and unexpected events. The feeling of running into somebody at the store you haven't seen for a long time. This is a fairly neutral card. It is generally a pleasant card and the other cards around it provide the emotion.
Four of Spades	Indicates illness or depression. The card cautions you about health and mental state. It's a depressing, gloomy, unhealthy card.
Five of Spades	Signifies anger. The feeling of red hot anger. Imagine a forest being burned down. Sometimes a good clearing of the air needs to happen for new growth to occur.
Six of Spades	Signifies caution, most of the time. This card is a warning to proceed slowly, hold back, keep certain emotions in reserve. *Sometimes* it indicates pregnancy.
Seven of Spades	Signifies loss. The feeling your dog is gone, purse is gone, job is gone, or lover is gone. It's gone and this card means the object of your affection is not coming back

Eight of Spades	Signifies tears. Imagine the feeling of pity, self-pity, sorrow, and crying cleansing, comforting, healing tears.
Nine of Spades	Signifies grief and anguish. This is the feeling of mourning. The period of longing for what can't be brought back. Unresolved heartaches.
Ten of Spades	Indicates a journey. There are no emotions related to this card, it simply means going out or coming off a journey.
Jack of Spades	Represents a young male, intellectual rather than emotional in how he views the world. He seeks justice and is judgmental by nature.
Queen of Spades	Represents a woman, mentally sharp and often considered to be aloof and not given to emotional gestures.
King of Spades	Represents a male, older in age or spirit. Trust his guidance, he has insight to help you find direction.
Ace of Spades	Conclusion, Ending; or Distance.
Upright	It means a conclusion, an ending, over. The death of circumstances. With death, there is always a new beginning. Death in card readings is a door. It's up to you to open the door and walk through to a new beginning.
Upside down/ reversed	The card is telling you about someone or something at a distance, usually quite far away. The other cards around it will tell you what is at a distance or what the message is.

Homework Practice

Shuffle both suits, Hearts and Spades, together, putting aside the rest of the deck. Deal out two sets of three cards each. Describe to yourself what these cards mean and what you feel about each three-card group.

Chapter Five
Learning the Suit of Diamonds

As you continue your study of Personal Prophesy with this lesson, you will have developed a beginning level of intuitive perception about three of the suits of the deck: Hearts, Spades and now, Diamonds.

No doubt you are beginning to *feel* the meanings of each of the cards as you expand your own intuitive perception. But if you still feel lost in terms of "reading" the cards, don't despair. While you are well on your way toward becoming a knowledgeable card reader, you still have more to learn. The following tips are designed to aid you in your steady progress.

1. **Concentrate on slow, steady progress.** This is a highly complex skill you are learning. Achieving the right perception of the cards and the proper method for reading them takes time and considerable effort in order to do it accurately.
2. **Remember, as you are learning that your perception is your own.** You will not intuitively feel the same meaning in the individual cards as other readers do, so try not to compare your perceptions to others who are also learning. Emotions are a lot like snowflakes – we don't all experience emotions in the same way and won't interpret them the same way, either.
3. **Practice, practice, practice.** There really is no way around it: The only way you will ever achieve accuracy with the cards is simply to practice whenever and wherever possible.

4. **Your level of intuitive perception will occasionally fluctuate.** It happens; one day you feel like a card reading virtuoso and then next, you can't seem to get any messages from them at all. Allow yourself these moments of inconsistency in your reading ability – sometimes we just aren't as in touch intuitively as we'd like to be. When you feel as if you can't read the cards, just put them away and try again later or the next day. A break can mean all the difference in the world in terms of your level of perception.

5. **Nothing in the cards should ever be considered to be cast in stone.** When you read the cards, you are essentially taking a slice of your life and momentarily examining it, perceiving it and re-defining it; but you must remember that the future is very fluid, still affected by change. What you see in the cards should be perceived as having strong potential for becoming reality. It doesn't necessarily mean it will be reality. There is a very big difference.

6. **Be extremely cautious when you first begin to read the cards for others.** A trainee in a professional medical environment would hardly be expected to be ready to perform major surgery but your friends and relatives will consider your Personal Prophesy internship to make you an instant master of intuitive perception. It will take at least six weeks for you to be capable of conducting a reading for someone else, but you'd be amazed how many of your first "clients" will hold you to what you tell them. So do be careful and keep the reading general.

7. **If one of your cards becomes bent or curled, that card has to go.** It may be okay to play Solitaire with a couple of weather-beaten cards in the deck, but my experience has been that these cards have no place in an honest-to-goodness intuitive reading. The cuts you make in the wishing process will not be correct. Even shuffling the cards will not seem genuine with bad cards in your hands. I save my old decks and use the good cards as replacements. All the bent, creased, curled cards are thrown away.

8. **Make it standard practice to count your cards before you do a reading.** The last thing you want to do is a reading with only 51 cards in your hands. Do ensure that you have all 52 every time you

go to read them. And yes, if you should happen to miscount the number of cards you take from the cuts, you do have start over.

9. **Shuffle the cards at least three times between each layout.** When you purchase a new deck, shuffle the cards, and shuffle again. It takes ten full shuffles to thoroughly mix a new deck of cards. For readings, I always shuffle the cards three times between layouts.

10. **Don't let skeptics get to you.** No matter who you are or where you go, you'll find yourself dealing with skeptics in one form or another. Learn the cards for yourself and no one else. If you believe they can help you lead a happier, more fulfilling life, that's all that matters. You will never bring skeptical people to the point of change in their way of thinking, nor will you ever convince them that you can read the cards. Make Personal Prophesy your special skill, your own window on the future and leave skepticism to those who aren't open to the limitless possibilities of the universe in the way that you are.

In this lesson, you will study the suit of Diamonds and the meanings of the individual cards contained in it. Diamonds are, by nature, cards that signify development, relationship and acquisition.

Two of Diamonds – Secretiveness

This means "secrets"… but you have to feel this card. Imagine you are looking at a person who is holding something behind their back. You don't know what it is or why they feel they have to hide it from you. Does that image make you feel suspicious? That feeling of suspicion is the essence of the card. This is a sneaky, secretive card.

It's letting you know that something important is being hidden from view and you should be wary when you see this card in your readings.

Three of Diamonds – Conflicts

This card literally means "domestic conflicts. You can feel it as if you and I had a length of rope between us and all of a sudden I jerk it.

Your response is to jerk right back, of course. Soon, we are pulling like fools attempting to jerk the rope more and more in our own direction, while becoming frustrated and essentially getting nowhere. This card indicates that a conflict can go from petty differences to major feud in no time at all.

When you see this card in your readings, it is telling you to find a way to make a workable peace in this situation, and soon.

Four of Diamonds – Lies

This can literally means "untrueness", it focuses on lies, infidelity, cheating, revenge, backstabbing.

The symbolism for this card you'll develop on your own. In terms of relationships it's a big time "cheating card". It tells you not to trust and to be very much on your guard when it appears in your readings. It's giving you the message that deceit and betrayal are afoot. Pay attention to this card. It imports a serious message in terms of Personal Prophesy philosophy.

Take the three Fours in the deck that you have learned so far and blend them together in your mind. The Four of Diamonds – Lies or cheating. The Four of Spades – Illness. The Four of Hearts – Jealousy. This is a true emotional crisis. It is an awful mix. If, say, you were cheating and reading your own cards, my experience says you would reference that "cheating" more with cards like "secrets", "caution", the "loss" and "grief" of Spades if you felt guilty. These three cards blended together would indicate more an emotional crisis in terms of learning that the one you love or care for deeply is betraying you. You will learn these subtle differences as you gain skill with the cards.

Five of Diamonds – News

This literally means "news". I see it as an ear receiving information. The cards connected to it will tell you whether it's good news or bad news. The Five of Diamonds is a neutral card in that it has no emotional message on its own, but it is, nonetheless, an important card in that it brings information to you within the context of the reading and lets you know that new developments are in the making.

Six of Diamonds – Relationship and Eight of Diamonds – Relationship

Both the Six and Eight of Diamonds mean "a relationship exists here", as in between family members, friends, co-workers. These two cards are considered to be neutral cards in that they have no emotional message on their own, they simply signify relationship.

The message about the relationship depends on where they are placed in the reading. If either one appears in front of a face card, it indicates your relationship with that individual. If either one appears to the immediate right of a face card, it indicates that individual's relationship with you. We will get into the placement of these two cards later. For now, just think "a relationship exists here".

Seven of Diamonds –Gossip, Scandal

This is your "scandal" card. It's gossipy, behind your back stuff. Let's think about "scandal" ... how much "scandal" is true... how much is not? I see this card in readings as if I were driving by a motel at noon and see a female acquaintance of mine coming out of a room with some guy. I don't know who that guy is, but the two of them are laughing and hugging. I think, "She must have spent the night with him." I run home and get on AOL and tell all of you about how she's cheating on her husband before I take the time to find out that the guy happens to be her brother visiting from back home.

Because I have drawn my own assumptions and acted on what I saw, I have created "scandal" for this female acquaintance. It's a very important message about misinterpreting what we see. This card will tell you that people are talking about you and defaming you as a result of false impressions.

This card falls under the category of "things you cannot change." You can only learn from this card that you might want to keep your business more to yourself.

Nine of Diamonds – Uncertainty

This is an easy card to learn. It literally means "uncertainty." It focuses on confusion and indecision. It tells you "the answer is still not decided." It can also tell you when a new partner is unsure of his or her feelings for you or if a boss is contemplating firing you.

We'll get into the more intricate meanings associated with this card later on. For now, just think that the Nine is a useful tool in all areas of your life, letting you know that you are being misunderstood, dealing with chaos all around you or in a situation for which the outcome has yet to be determined.

Ten of Diamonds – Money

This card means "money" and signifies financial matters. It's another neutral card in the deck in that it has no emotional message on its own.

Diamonds people are characterized as being somewhat materialistic, money-minded. They are often great performers, and can be on the egotistical side in certain respects because they enjoy being in the limelight. They may also be business owners, investment brokers/bankers, tax consultants. They are somewhat cold by nature, aloof, difficult to know.

The Ace of Diamonds – Merger

The Ace signifies "unity" as in marriage, mergers, partnerships. It indicates a very strong bond, a commitment to a goal or purpose, a meeting of minds. It can definitely indicate a wedding between romantic partners. Think "unity" in your readings when the Ace appears.

A Summary of the Suit of Diamonds

Here are simple descriptions for the Suit of Diamonds. These descriptions are only intended to help you generate an image in your own mind of that card's essence... allow yourself to feel the flow of intuitive thought for each card.

Two of Diamonds	Signifies secrets and the feeling of suspicion, as if somebody is hiding something from you behind their back.
Three of Diamonds	Signifies petty, domestic conflicts. Tug of war between people. Signals small disagreements that could escalate into more serious disputes.
Four of Diamonds	Signifies cheating, lies, deception, infidelity.
Five of Diamonds	Indicates news. It simply means you are going to hear some news. This card is neutral; the other cards surrounding it will tell you the nature of that news.
Six of Diamonds	Indicates that a relationship exists. A neutral card, the other cards around this Six of Diamonds will tell you what kind of relationship.
Seven of Diamonds	Signifies scandal. This card represents gossip and irresponsible rumours being circulated.
Eight of Diamonds	Identical to the Six of Diamonds in meaning, it indicates that a relationship exists.
Nine of Diamonds	Signifies uncertainty. This card has no negative feelings associated with it, although it can signify that someone is uncertain of their feelings for you. It simply means a decision about the matter in question has not been made.
Ten of Diamonds	Indicates money and financial matters. Another neutral card.
Ace of Diamonds	Represents partnership, merger. The card signifies marriage and situations like a marriage, such as a partnership, merger, solid agreement. See it as a very strong union or unity.
Jack of Diamonds	Represents a young materialistic male.
Queen of Diamonds	Represents a female who enjoys spending, acquiring possessions.
King of Diamonds	Represents an older male, who may work in finance or who is interested in financial matters and determining value.

Homework Practice

Shuffle the three suits you have now learned: Hearts, Spades and Diamonds, with the Clubs discarded. Deal out nine cards into three groups containing three cards each. Concentrate on what you "feel" about the cards in these groups. In other words, perceive them in groups of three and also, as an overall picture of the nine cards in general.

Chapter Six
Learning the Suit of Clubs

When you read the cards, remember that your emotions, as you are experiencing them at that particular moment, will influence your readings considerably. Try to sit down with a clear, open mind whenever you conduct a reading – you will achieve a much more accurate reading in the long run.

Here are some additional tips to help you learn to read the cards for yourself and others more effectively:

1. Bear in mind that the cards are revealing to you situations as they intuitively appear **at that particular moment** when you are conducting a reading. Change has the power to alter your readings at any time and you should read the cards with the awareness that such fluctuations may occur. In other words, nothing in the cards is ever "written in stone".

2. When you read the cards, they are only *advising* you about the future and aren't *directing* your life path in any way. The insight you gain from them is intended to guide you in decision-making about your life, but the course you ultimately take is one that belongs only to you.

3. When you perceive negative situations developing in the cards, don't fear them but focus on doing what you can to **change the circumstances** involved before these situations become reality.

By preparing yourself for them, you are taking steps to alter these situations for the better before they even occur.

4. When you read the cards for others, always describe the futures you perceive with compassion and care. Remember that those you are conducting readings for don't possess the knowledge that you do at this point and, more times than not, are extremely apprehensive about having their futures perceived in this way.

5. Don't reveal more in your readings than you feel the recipients of them can emotionally handle as you conduct them. Not everyone is prepared to accept dramatic change or can comprehend in one sitting the deep insights about their own lives that you are capable of perceiving. Lead them slowly to your level of awareness by gently guiding them toward the best path you see for them to take toward the future.

6. Decline to read the cards for highly skeptical people. No matter how accurate your perceptions may be intuitively about their lives, they will only insist you are wrong and this can shake your confidence.

7. Remember when you read the cards that the emotions of others as you perceive them may not be consciously recognized by these people. We are all living life on a level far different from each other. Some of us are in touch with our emotions and others are not. You are perceiving the intricate workings of their own hearts and cannot force anyone to acknowledge feelings they aren't aware even exist at that particular point in time.

8. Always search for hope in your readings. It is ever-present. Your task is to search it out, as you conduct your readings, from among the trouble and heartache you perceive in the cards.

Our emotions are constantly evolving. What we perceive about them today may not be the same perception we have of them tomorrow. Allow room for personal growth in your readings. When you do, you will find yourself becoming far wiser and more capable of handling change, which is inherent to emotion, in the long run.

Chances are, you will find the fourth, and final, suit contained in the deck relatively easy to understand.

I tend to consider Clubs to be "vehicle cards" when I read them. On the intuitive level, they contain aspects which tend to relate to activity or movement in terms of psychological experience.

Two of Clubs – Minor Disappointment

This card literally means "disappointment" – minor disappointment, as in, things didn't go exactly as you had hoped or planned. Don't associate this card with any of the heavy feelings attached to the cards in the suit of Spades. Those cards indicate huge, emotions. The emotion connected to this card is very small. It isn't a terribly meaningful card in most instances. But if say, you had planned to meet a friend or expected to go out to dinner with someone, this card would let you know whether those plans would materialize and if the experience would be what you expected it to be.

If your reading told you, "You're going to be a little disappointed with this experience," then you could prepare in advance for that disappointment.

Three of Clubs – Creation

This is a very complicated card until you are able to fully understand it. This card is one of the most important cards in the deck. It literally means "creation".

The Three of Clubs is alerting you to a moment in time taking shape which has very strong potential for becoming reality (which is a rather heavy concept).

Imagine this card as a hard little ball soaring through space, and it's coming right at you. If that ball hits you, it's going to hit you, hard. It won't necessarily hit you with pain, but it is going to hit you in terms of "impact". In other words, you will feel that ball striking you, one way or the other.

That ball is, intuitively speaking, a future moment the cards are trying to tell you is "coming right at you". According to Personal Prophesy, you have some choices to make about that ball. You can turn around and be ready to catch it in your hands when it finally reaches you. You can run and hide from it. You can choose to ignore it and let it knock you off your feet when it hits you.

Keep the number '3' in mind when you see this card in your readings. It's very important in terms of that reading. This card is letting you know that an event is taking shape to become reality in your life in a period of time represented by the number '3'– three days, three weeks, three months...

Here's the really deep message attached to this card: Numbers have meanings, in and of themselves. Number 1 means 'unity'. Number 2 means 'opposition'. If you think about number 1 being like a stick just standing there, it is united in its singularity. Number 2 would be two sticks standing there and they signify 'opposite'. Number 3 means 'creation': two sticks (representing opposition) and a new stick developing from those two sticks.

This card is a difficult card to teach in terms of its deep meaning, but it will become one of your favourites in readings. I guarantee it.

Four of Clubs – Misfortune

This is a card you will find your own personal meaning for. It is literally translated as "misfortune", but you must decipher for yourself what exactly" misfortune" is within the framework of your own life.

You may see this card in your readings as if you were making a trip to the store and you suddenly have to take a detour, as a result of road works being done which alters your pre-planned course. This detour causes you to be late, perhaps you lose your way and miss an appointment. In essence, you must make sudden and unexpected adjustments in your life at that precise moment.

Some see this card as a terrible accident on the highway and having to narrowly escape becoming involved in it. The card, plainly speaking, means "misfortune". Call it your Murphy's Law card, "The worst possible thing that could happen at the worst possible time."

You will find your own interpretation for "misfortune" as you learn to read the cards.

Five of Clubs – an Agreement

This card simply indicates "an agreement." See it as two people shaking hands. It relates to contracts, deals, proposals being accepted, going steady with someone, sharing the same point of view. It's a very good card all by itself.

Six of Clubs – Effort

This is a card that means "effort" particularly in connection to your work and the workplace. It can actually mean "the workplace" in certain instances. This is another neutral card in readings. It simply means "effort" or "work" and the cards which join it in a reading will define it in terms of emotion and its intuitive message for you.

Seven of Clubs – Sexual Attraction

This is a card which signifies "sexual attraction". Its primary focus is on getting that attraction gratified. Men tend to view their attractions to women on this level initially. You must always advise women to be watchful of this when you conduct readings for them. Men are not interested in "falling in love" when they are simply attracted sexually. They are being led to satisfy that sexual urge.

A woman needs to learn how to use this desire for sex to her benefit. She needs to use that urge for sexual gratification by making him care for her on another level before she gratifies his urge.

Because women are more often emotionally drawn in their attractions, they are more led from the heart. I have read for some very promiscuous women in the past, even some who were "professional gals", and even they are searching for love, but going about it from an entirely wrong aspect in their relationships with men.

When you see this card in your readings, be aware of its intuitive meaning: The drive for sexual gratification and nothing more.

Eight of Clubs – Frustration

This is a card that literally means "frustration." You might visualize this card as if you were standing in line at the grocery store and the person in front of you is buying a great many things and you feel frustrated at having to wait, as you want to get out of the store. Or a traffic jam that is bringing your journey to a halt.

My own personal interpretation of this card is "constipation", because it signifies a blockage of some kind. You can't seem to get around it, no matter how hard you try. You can't ignore that blockage, either. You simply have to deal with your feelings of frustration.

See this card in your readings as "more effort is needed" in terms of a certain situation, and even then, it might not come out right. That is the essence of this card.

Nine of Clubs – Indulgence

This is a card which focuses on "indulgence": drinking, smoking, partying, eating, even drug use. In certain contexts, it merely indicates "enjoying and indulging". In others, it means "addiction" and "abuse". You will learn to know the difference as you advance your intuitive ability. For now, just think, "indulging."

Ten of Clubs – Officialdom

This is a card that represents "official" things and it's also a card concerned with business activity. This card is neutral, it simply means business, government, legal matters. In some instances it will convey to you that one of your people cards wears a uniform.

The Ace of Clubs – Communication

This is a card of Communication. Clubs are almost all neutral cards. This card indicates making and receiving significant phone calls, letters.

Face cards, as you get to know them and progress with this training, will tell you intuitively who people are in your life as you conduct your readings. Clubs face cards are those in the category of being the workers or inventors in life. Those represented by Clubs face cards in your readings are those who generally advance society in the work they do and the dreams they dream.

Summary of The Suit of Clubs

Two of Clubs	Indicates minor disappointments where expectations are concerned. This card translates as "The outcome will not be quite as anticipated."
Three of Clubs	Signifies "duration of time"; an event coming right at you. Imagine standing in one place and a hard ball is soaring through space, coming at you. Your back is turned and it's going to hit you hard. But if you turn around and get ready for it, you will be able to catch it. This is the essence of the Three of Clubs. The number "3" is significant with this card, it can mean 3 hours, 3 days, 3 weeks, 3 months...
Four of Clubs	Signifies misfortune. This card warns of a major setback, an unexpected set of circumstances that must be prepared for.
Five of Clubs	Indicates an agreement, contracts, deals, commitments, transactions.
Six of Clubs	Represents effort. It focuses on work or the workplace.
Seven of Clubs	Signifies desire and sexual attraction. This card does not represent affection, simply the sexual attraction seeking gratification.
Eight of Clubs	Indicates frustration and impatience.
Nine of Clubs	Signifies indulgence. This card represents drinking, drugs, over-eating, over-socializing, at its worst. Having a good time, enjoying the company of others in a social atmosphere are its more positive aspects.
Ten of Clubs	Indicates something "official." This card is neutral and focuses on legalities, government or military matters.
Jack of Clubs	Represents a younger male who is idealistic by nature.
Queen of Clubs	Represents a female who is extremely creative and inventive.
King of Clubs	Represents a male who is older in age or "spirit" with spontaneous wit and sharp intelligence.
Ace of Clubs	Indicates Communication: phone calls, letters, online interaction. It is also a neutral card.

Homework Practice

Deal out two groups of three cards using all the suits you have learned. Read each group, focusing on what you feel about the cards in these groups. Repeat this exercise as often as necessary until you are comfortable with the suits of the deck.

Chapter Seven
Arranging the Cards for a Reading

Congratulations!

You have reached the point in your instruction where you are now ready to actually learn to read the cards for yourself and, with enough practice, for others who would like to receive a reading from you.

In order to accomplish that, you must now learn how to properly arrange the cards for conducting your readings. The arrangement is called layout. There are a variety of card-reading layouts out there (as you will discover if you do any research on the subject in the library), but this is one I mainly use for Personal Prophesy readings. While it may seem complicated to remember in the beginning, I assure you that with time and practice you'll be arranging the cards in this layout like an expert.

The Personal Prophesy Layout: Step-by-Step

1. Count your cards and shuffle your deck. If it is a new deck, be sure to shuffle it at least 10 times to properly mix the cards. If it is already well-mixed, three thorough shuffles between layouts should be sufficient for producing accurate readings.

2. Place the deck on the table in front of you and as you think intently about the Wish or Question you would like the cards to give you insight on, use your left hand to cut the deck once, so

that you have two piles of cards on the table in front of you. (According to my grandmother's teachings, the left hand is always used in cutting the cards because it is the one closest to your heart.)

3. Make a cut in the second pile, so that you now have three separate piles of cards on the table in front of you: 1 2 3

4. Pick up pile #1 and count off 7 cards. Place these 7 cards on the table in front of you. Now take the 8th card from pile #1 still in your hand and place it, face UP, several inches above the 7 cards you counted off on the table, calling this Card A. Discard the remaining cards in your hand.

5. Pick up pile #2, again count off 7 cards, placing these 7 on top of the 7 you counted off from pile #1. Now take the 8th card from this pile in your hand, placing it face UP to the immediate RIGHT of Card A, calling this Card B. Discard the remaining cards in your hand.

6. Pick up pile #3, again count off 7 cards, placing these 7 on top of the 14 cards you previously counted off from piles #1 and #2. Now take the 8th card from the pile in your hand, placing it face UP to the immediate LEFT of Card A. Discard the remaining cards in your hand.

   The row of 3 cards you have arranged would look like this on the table in front of you: C A B

7. Now, pick up the 21 cards you have counted off and placed in a pile on the table in front of you. These are the cards you will complete your layout with in order to conduct your reading. The remaining cards of the deck that have been discarded will not be needed or used until you shuffle the whole deck to create a new layout.

8. Take the first card from the TOP of the 21 cards you have in your hand and, calling it Card D, place it below and diagonally to the LEFT of Card C. Following the letters of the alphabet for each consecutive card off the TOP after Card D, arrange them in the following order. Your layout will look like this when you are finished:

```
C A B
D L S      E M T      F N U      G O V
H P W      I Q X      J R ◄─── K
```

9. As the arrow indicates, move Card K closer toward Card R, so that it also is part of a three-card spread.

10. To read each spread (each series of three cards – there are 8 spreads in this layout) you begin with the card on the LEFT in that spread. For instance, with the top spread, you would read Card C first, then combine it with what you read from Card A, then combine both with what you read from Card B. You always read the cards left to right as if the spread was a mathematical equation: $1+1+1=$___. The sum total of that spread becomes the Personal Prophesy message you receive from it.

Spread Designations

The Personal Prophesy layout you are learning in this lesson contains eight separate spreads – in other words, 8 distinctly separate 3-card combinations. Each of these 3-card combinations have designations, which you will learn as you continue with your training, represent 8 different areas in your life (or the life of the person you are conducting the reading for) which you should consider in very loose, fluid terms when you come to read the cards in the layout.

  These designations are:

1. Cards C A B: These three cards refer to the present moment or the atmosphere surrounding your life right now.

2. Cards D L S: These three cards refer to your home or the home situation.

3. Cards E M T: These cards refer to yourself or matters most important to you.

4. Cards F N U: These cards refer to your wish – the question you posed to the cards when you cut the deck for the reading.

The Nine of Hearts can appear anywhere in the layout, but this particular spread will pertain to your wish and will provide you with extra information about the wish you are making.

5. Cards G O V: These cards refer to matters or circumstances you don't expect at this particular time. This spread alerts to you events that could occur outside of your immediate expectations.
6. Cards H P W: These cards refer to matters or circumstances you do expect and provide you with some additional information regarding them.
7. Cards I Q X: These cards fall into the designation "what will surprise you" and indicate circumstances you should prepare yourself for in the future.
8. Cards J R K: These cards fall into the designation "what is sure to come true" and indicate situations and/or circumstances you should pay special attention to because they are rather fixed in nature and are unlikely to change before they become reality.

Bear in mind that these are not rigid designations, only personal guides in the layout. Once you've learned them, they will become second nature to you as you read the entire layout.

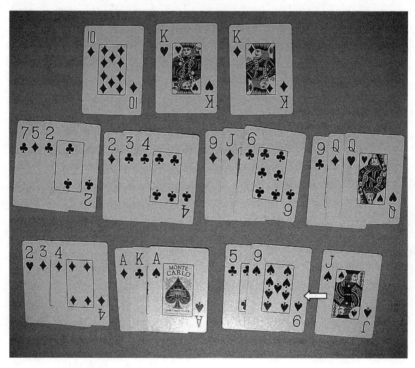

Homework Practice

Focus on learning the layout by practicing placing the cards in order. Don't extend yourself by trying to "read" the cards until you are comfortable with laying down the cards in this layout for a reading. Once you can arrange the layout without referring to the diagram, then you can begin to concentrate on reading the cards in each spread. If you practice daily, you should have no problem shuffling and placing the cards in the layout without the diagram in a week's time or less.

The Technical Side to Card Reading

If you feel rather confused at this point, you have good reason to feel that way. You have just received a tremendous amount of information which you have yet to process fully – intellectually and intuitively. This "processing" only comes with time. The more you practice with your cards and gain personal knowledge about them, the more you devote yourself to concentrating on developing that ever-important intuitive link with your cards – individually and collectively in the layout – the more you will process the information that you've received with each and every day that passes.

This lesson will teach you more about the technical side to reading the cards. I intentionally withheld this information from the previous lessons so that you would not find yourself faced with too much to digest all at once. Learning the intuitive meanings of 52 cards and the Personal Prophesy layout is more than enough of a challenge for the true beginner.

Now you are no longer a "true beginner". You are a "novice card reader," well on your way to conducting accurate intuitive readings with those 52 cards you hold in your hands.

Let's explore the card reading process on a deeper level now. This information will help you achieve greater clarity in your readings as we fine-tune your personal knowledge and advancing skills in terms of Personal Prophesy.

The word layout, refers to the 24-card arrangement you learned in the last lesson. Within the layout, there are 8 different spreads – the individual 3-card series of cards you read once the layout for the reading has been arranged.

When you read the cards in the 8 spreads of the layout, you think of yourself as experiencing the cards from left to right in each of the spreads. That means you are always to the left side in a reading. Visualize yourself as being on the "receiving end" of the cards in each of the spreads in your layout.

When you read the cards in each spread, you follow a 1+1+1= ___ equation. Begin to read that spread with the first card in this 3-card series by concentrating on perceiving the message of that first card.

As an example, suppose the Nine of Spades is that first card. Allow yourself time to intuitively "feel" the pain, the grief symbolized by that card. When you have successfully accomplished that, turn to the second card in that particular spread.

Let's suppose the second card is the Seven of Spades. Concentrate on the intuitive message contained in that card: Loss. Once you've felt the meaning symbolized by that card, blend it with the first card. Pain + Loss is what you have so far. Blend these emotions inside yourself. Feel them, separately and together.

These emotions are perceived as being experienced by yourself in the future, because they lay in the spread in front of a face card. Had these cards fallen in the reading behind a face card these emotions would belong to the individual represented by that card. When there are no face cards in a spread, all three cards indicate emotions which belong only to you.

Now, move on to the third card. Let's say this card is the Ace of Diamonds. Look at this card and experience its intuitive meaning: Marriage, a strong union. Following the "1+1+1" equation, go back to the first card, blend it emotionally with the second card and now blend both of them with the third card.

What you are perceiving would appear in your intuitive mind as:

$$\text{Pain} + \longrightarrow \text{Loss} + \longrightarrow \text{Marriage} =$$
$$\text{(the intuitive message of the spread)}$$

If these cards appeared in a spread in your own reading, they would be sending you the message: "Prepare to experience intense grief over the loss of your partner."

Do you see how I arrived at that message? If not, I guarantee that you will, in time. At this point, only focus on getting that intuitive equation right, on being able to read the cards in each of the spreads as $1+1+1=$___.

Let's move on to face cards, the people cards in your readings. There are a number of intricate innuendos attached to the face cards – don't try to learn them all in one sitting. In time, you will grasp these innuendos and come to understand the face cards very well in your readings.

The direction in which the actual faces on the face cards are turned means a great deal. If the face on a face card in a spread is looking left, this indicates that the individual represented by this card is turned toward you. Remember that you are always on the left in terms of a spread. The cards are giving you information about your life, or when you are conducting a readings for others, they are on the left and the cards are giving you intuitive messages about their lives.

If the face on the face card is looking to the right, this indicates that the individual represented by this card is turned away from you. When the face of a face card is turned toward you in a spread, it means that individual is literally looking at you, he or she is focused on the relationship shared with you, is extremely sensitive to your needs, and receptive about heading toward the future with you.

When the face of a face card is turned away from you in a spread, it means this individual's focus is elsewhere – they are not as concerned about the relationship you share, may not be particularly sensitive to your needs, or could be unreceptive about moving toward the future with you.

The direction of the faces on the face cards also gives you information about how these people live their lives in general. Those faces which look to the left, indicate individuals who derive their present-day emotions and perspectives on life in general from what they have learned from the past. The past, psychologically speaking, is considered to be to the left of us.

Those faces which look to the right, indicate individuals who derive their present-day emotions and perspectives on life overall by concentrating on the future. The future is, psychologically speaking, considered to be to the right of us.

The Wishing Process

When you shuffle and cut the cards, making a wish for knowledge on the cards – whether it's to know if someone in your life truly loves you or whether you will be offered a particular job you are seeking, the Nine of Hearts – the "Wish card" – will provide you with intuitive knowledge about what you are wishing for, at that particular moment in time.

When the Nine of Hearts falls favorably in a spread in your reading, it is indicating that what you wish for has potential for becoming reality based on circumstances at that present time. When the Nine of Hearts falls unfavorably in a spread in your reading, it is indicating that what you wish for does not have potential for becoming reality based on circumstances at the present time.

Bear in mind that life fluctuates; everyday circumstances are affected by change. What may not be perceived in a reading today as having potential for becoming reality, could easily change by tomorrow.

This is the reason why I urge new students to read the cards for themselves at least once a day. By doing so, you have the opportunity to see potential for the future literally change before your eyes. You also have the opportunity to prepare for personal setbacks – those things you wish for which do not have potential for becoming reality – because you gain pre-knowledge about these wishes. How do you gain this pre-knowledge? By reading the cards on a routine, daily basis which will only make your own personal, intuitive link to them that much stronger in the end.

Wishful Thinking

I have provided intuitive guidance over the years for countless people who have one major problem in common. In every case, they were madly in love with someone who the cards consistently indicated were not true, faithful, caring partners.

These people couldn't seem to understand why they were so miserable, yet the reality of the situation they were in was staring them in the face. The relationships they were pinning all of their hopes and dreams to were not going to succeed, no matter how hard they might try to make it so. The prophesy was there, it was just a simple case of futile wishful thinking to avoid having to accept the inevitable.

The message of the cards for men and women who are enduring disastrous love relationships will always be the same, even though so few are willing to listen: "*Stop clinging to partners who are incapable of making you happy.*"

What is it about the human heart that makes us put so much energy into loving people who are never going to love us back? The cards will show you who is incapable of loving you back. You will also know beyond a shadow of a doubt who can be a faithful partner, deserving of your love, *if* you listen to the intuitive messages contained in your reading.

In order for you to achieve the kind of happiness in love that you hope for, you will have to do one important thing right now: Accept the reality of your situation as it exists this very moment. You must be completely honest with yourself and realize that the cards reflect how things realistically appear and not merely how you wish they could be.

Wishing is an important part of the card reading process. When you get a reading, you are in essence wishing on the cards for knowledge: to determine how close or how far you actually are from the things you want; whether there are unexpected difficulties ahead that will have to be dealt with; and what circumstances and individuals will be encountered – who may all bring changes to the path you have chosen to happiness. This kind of wishing is extremely important to your ability to get what you need and desire in love and friendship.

Wishful thinking, however, is a grand illusion that what you want to be true is true and ultimately puts you at the mercy of the choices made by the people living their lives around you.

If you tend to find yourself on the losing end of your relationships, now is the time for you to do something about it. By accepting the reality of your situation (which is not to be confused with simply accepting the situation "as is" and living with it, something you don't have to do), you are seeing your life as it really is and taking the first step toward resolution and change – change that Personal Prophesy will show you is a powerful, creative force when used properly.

Are you single and lonely? Single and involved in a relationship that is not making you happy, wondering if there might be somebody better for you out there? Perhaps you're married, but spending life with a partner who doesn't satisfy your needs, or you aren't completely sure this is a partner you can really trust?

None of these "realities" are permanent, although we have all been conditioned to think of them as such when they're actually happening to us. But remember, life is change, whether those changes are on a physical, intellectual, or emotional level. The cards will constantly be filled with possibilities for these changes to alter your situation and, consequently, the rest of your life.

The possibilities that are forever present in the cards are definite viable options that you can choose or refuse at will, putting you in control of what happens to you, giving you confidence, without the need for wishful thinking and other illusionary traps.

Homework Practice

Create a 3-card spread of your choice, using the 1+1+1= ___ equation, which illustrates that a face card is "turned toward" you. Create another spread which illustrates that a face card is turned away from you and do a reading of each spread. Repeat as necessary until you feel comfortable with these concepts. Consider what you perceive from your cards and determine whether you see any potential situations involving wishful thinking on your part or that of someone else in your life.

Chapter Eight
Understanding Intuitive Imagery

Should you find yourself still feeling confused about certain aspects of the Personal Prophesy material you've been studying so far, or you feel you are so overwhelmed that you aren't quite sure what you've actually learned about intuitively reading cards, don't despair. You are much further along in terms of expanding your own intuitive perception than you may think.

Most new students, I've found, are far too hard on themselves when they perceive their own overall performance. They tend to be terrible taskmasters who demand nothing short of pure perfection of themselves during their own practice sessions or whenever they attempt to conduct intuitive readings for others.

Such a performance-driven mind-set will not make you a better card reader, I'm afraid, only a severely frustrated one. I urge you not to harshly judge your ability at this point, but rather, congratulate yourself. Pat yourself on the back. If you only knew how many give up before they even reach the completion of all that you have thus far, you would realize just how much you have accomplished, how far you've come as a result of your own determination to stick-to-it.

In essence, you have taken brand-new steps toward self-awareness and personal enlightenment which will make it possible for you to run, intuitively, later on. Ask yourself: Would you honestly stand a one-year-old infant on his or her feet and say, "Now, run to the other side of the room?" Hardly. You'd be thrilled to see that child have the courage to take even three tentative baby steps away from you.

This is how you must visualize your own expansion of intuitive perception. During the past several lessons, you have focused on learning the intuitive meanings of 52 cards, and the Personal Prophesy layout. You have learned some basics about Personal Prophesy. That is a lot to absorb this quickly! Much of what you've learned took me years to fully understand. I concentrated on allowing myself the time and patience to learn, to absorb, to take those baby-sized steps into a gi-ant, brand-new world. If you do the same, you will one day be able to intuitively run as a result of those tiny steps. I guarantee it.

Three New Technical Details

The following three points were saved so they wouldn't unnecessarily trip you up or cause you further confusion as you focused on your learning process.

1. When two cards that bear the same number fall together in a spread, this indicates that the intuitive message you are receiving from those two cards in the spread is intensified. For example, consider this spread:

    Two of Hearts   Two of Spades   Six of Hearts

    The Two of Hearts, you've learned, indicates accomplishment and happiness through realized dreams. The Two of Spades is intuitively perceived as Change. When you combine those two cards and then look to the third card in the spread, Six of Hearts: a bright road leading toward the future – this spread is conveying a very strong, positive message: "Continue to follow your professional dream and approaching Change will develop into an even more productive path to take into the future."

2. When all three cards bearing the same number fall together in a spread, this indicates that the intuitive message you are receiving from those two cards in the spread is even more intensified. For example, consider this spread, a more negatively arranged one:

Four of Hearts   Four of Diamonds   Four of Clubs

This is an intensified emotional situation, all right. In fact, it's a downright emotional crisis. You've got jealousy, untrueness and misfortune to perceive here and with them all together it means in simple terms, "Prepare for an intensely-upsetting setback emotionally which will take some time for you to resolve and recover from."

3. Whenever the Tens of the suits come together in two's or three's in a spread, these are indicators of dynamic, sweeping, wonderful change. When the Tens are coupled or tripled view them as "rocket ships to the moon" in terms of their prophesy for success, money, love, travel. These are beautiful, beautiful cards in readings and you should definitely look for them, always.

More Detailed Information Regarding the Reading Layout

Now that you've mastered the Personal Prophesy layout and have achieved a certain amount of expertise in intuitively reading the cards on your own, let's learn a few more in-depth aspects involved in the reading process.

The Layout Designations:

1. **Your Current Situation:** When you view the uppermost spread in your reading, this designation provides you with intuitive information about your life in general at the time you are conducting your reading.

   The word "current" in this context means your life at that very moment. At times, this spread will seem quite meaningless to you, like a riddle you don't fully understand. Other times, you will know immediately the cards contained in this spread are reflecting aspects you are already aware of about your current situation, offering you even greater insight in the process.

   When you find the Nine of Hearts appearing in this spread, it is letting you know the intuitive answer to the question you posed to the cards for that particular reading, is a cut-and-dried, one-way-or-the-other response. This spread provides you with immediate, timely information relating to right now, this very moment, in terms of your life and its current direction.

Considerable insight is contained in this spread but do take it with a grain of salt as you read it. After all, the present is as fluid as the future at times; what you see in this spread today can easily change by tomorrow. Still, such insight is invaluable, as we are essentially living our lives moment-to-moment. The more we can learn about the moment, the better the cards can guide us in our decision-making for the future.

2. **To Your Home:** This designation encompasses matters relating to and having the power to impact your home emotionally, economically, spiritually. For instance, family relationships, children, domestic issues, close friends, work situations you literally take home with you.

    Bear in mind when you read the cards contained in this spread that, intuitively speaking, your "home" isn't necessarily where you physically keep your clothes and personal belongings. On the intuitive level, your "home" is that place where you feel "at home" in the emotional sense.

    You may live 1,000 miles from the place you truly consider to be "your home", as in the location where you were born and raised. Your "home" may be the office where you feel most comfortable and secure about yourself. Where you live when you are not in your office is another place entirely. Your "home" may be onboard a ship or in a cherished far-off place you routinely visit. It can even be a precious, personal interpretation of what you envision your true "home" spiritually to be.

    Home, therefore, should be interpreted when you read this spread as place relative to where your heart feels most secure and complete. It doesn't necessarily involve the building in which you live. The more you take this into account in your readings, the better your perception of the future as it pertains to "Your Home" will become.

3. **To Yourself:** This designation in the reading layout focuses on you – your hopes, dreams, goals for the future, beliefs and values, your emotional makeup, and personal identity – "who" you are essentially as a person as you live your life day by day. However, sometimes this designation will point out that what we believe is true about ourselves as individuals is only a facade in terms of the real individual who lurks within.

For instance, you may think you are an extremely loving, giving person, but cards in this spread could reveal to you that all the loving and giving you pour so much of your energy into every day is actually based on deep-rooted insecurity about yourself and your relationships expressing itself through such acts of selflessness.

You might consider yourself to be a lackluster, talentless individual doomed to spend your life working in menial occupations, only to find cards in this spread urging you to follow your deepest career dreams because true success does indeed have the potential to become a serious reality within the framework of your life.

Keep an eye on this spread as you conduct your readings. It will offer you an abundance of information into your true self, "who" you are and what you are made of, as you go about the business of living your life from day to day.

4. **To Your Wish:** This designation in the reading layout is dedicated entirely to your wish – that specific question requesting intuitive knowledge which you pose to the cards whenever you decide to conduct a reading.

Never disregard the cards that appear in this spread, even when the Nine of Hearts is not contained in the reading layout as a whole. As disconnected as the messages of these cards may occasionally seem to be at the time you view them, they actually offer you vitally significant information about your wish (the question you've posed) for that particular reading.

Often you will find critical background information offered

to you in this designation. Details about the people or circumstances which are significantly attached to your wish. Future events prophesied long before they ever take shape in terms of reality. Pay special attention to this spread; the information contained in it has a very important reason for being there.

When you find the Nine of Hearts appears in this designation, view this as a strong intuitive sign that your wish for knowledge (or for a certain event to occur) is within your grasp. If the Nine of Hearts appears in another spread in the layout, read that spread, of course, but do make sure you also read this one as having a very close connection to your wish in general.

For example, suppose you have asked as your wish to know how a certain individual feels about you. The Nine of Hearts appears in a different spread in the layout, advising you intuitively that this person isn't quite sure what his or her actual feelings for you are. This spread would also be connected to that particular wish, offering you deeper intuitive information about that person's uncertainty.

You might find in this designation that this individual is still emotionally focused on a previous partner who caused tremendous heartache in the past. Or great caution may be perceived on his or her part as a result of feeling fearful because your moves have been too aggressive to that point. Or this person might actually be involved with someone else, without having openly told you.

Receiving this information makes it possible to intuitively get a behind the scenes view in terms of various relationships and situations in your life. You may even glimpse a few of your own unconscious motives coming through in this designation in regard to these situations.

When the Nine of Hearts does not appear anywhere in the reading layout, do still read this designation – particularly if the Nine does not appear during three separate layouts with the same wish for knowledge.

The cards contained in this designation will hold some very

clear intuitive information for you as to why that wish for knowledge is not to be answered in that particular reading.

I consider this "To Your Wish" designation to be the most significant in terms of insight in the layout for a reading. It offers volumes intuitively into the "story behind the story". This designation is devoted to imparting nothing but the truth for those who sincerely wish to seek it.

5. **What You Don't Expect:** What you don't expect is a designation in the reading which implies events and situations perceived to hold the potential to develop unexpectedly, which may impact your life both in a positive and negative sense. However, by possessing this knowledge in advance you put yourself at a great advantage, in the position of not being caught unaware should your course to the future continue to keep you on a collision course with such "unexpected events and situations".

For example, if you were to perceive your own committed partner in this spread as beginning to experience doubts about your relationship or perhaps feeling attracted to someone else, you would have the opportunity to take constructive action toward changing that prophesy for the future while living in the present. You could choose to initiate better communication between you. Put more energy into keeping your partner happy and satisfied. You could emotionally prepare yourself for his/her attraction to someone else to develop into something more meaningful in the future or decide to open yourself to new opportunity with someone else.

Much can be learned, intuitively, from this designation in the layout. The cards contained in it prepare you for the unexpected – although, don't be surprised if the other designations do so as well, from time to time.

6. **What You Do Expect:** This designation encompasses those aspects of life which we define in terms of our own personal ex-

pectations as we live our lives. Essentially it is that we can expect to live out our lives day-by-day.

For you, this designation may take on a whole new meaning as you progress in your study of Personal Prophesy. Your definition of the word "expectation" could be vastly different from mine. This is where your own interpretation of terms is crucial to your own individual reading process.

If you maintain a broad view in terms of what you "expect" from life, this designation will offer you all sorts of interesting, intuitive observations about your life and those in it. If you are more restrictive, those observations will be more limited. I feel very much the same way about the next layout designation:

7. **What is Sure to Surprise You:** Here again, an entirely individual interpretation is involved. What may surprise me, may not surprise you at all. Therefore, be fluid in your definition of these two designations and you will achieve far greater success with your cards in the end.

When you maintain a "sky's the limit" point of view in defining such words as "expectation" and "surprise", you open yourself to a wide variety of intuitive experience the Universe has to offer us. If you limit yourself, naturally, what you perceive from the cards contained in these designations will be just as limiting intuitively.

I can tell you that if I were to pick a specific designation from which miracles are often perceived in readings, it would definitely be this one. The cards contained in this spread will reveal to you some truly impossible and wondrous things if you are open enough intuitively to receive these prophesies when they appear in your readings. This is the designation which would, more than any other, pertain to "the impossible becoming possible", so do keep that aspect in mind when you read the cards it contains in your readings.

8. **What is Sure to Come True:** From this designation, you have

the ability to learn, to grow and ultimately, to achieve greater wisdom for yourself as a result of certain inevitabilities you will perceive from the cards contained in this spread.

You might consider this to be your "Destiny Spread" in readings, for the cards you find here prophesy events and circumstances which, realistically speaking, cannot be changed as you currently travel your life's path toward the future.

For instance, when a relationship is destined to meet its end, you will perceive its conclusion from the cards contained in this spread, often long before this ending actually occurs. When a relationship intended to bring new meaning and direction to your life is on its way to you, you will also perceive it here, months – if not years – in advance.

New career paths take shape as a result of this designation; the birth of children; the passing away of loved ones. Unfaithfulness, the loss of friendships, the making of new, more lasting friendships, divorces, marriages can all be prophesied from this designation in the reading layout.

If you give this designation a tremendous amount of weight in terms of your readings, you put yourself in an extremely powerful position intuitively. Doing so enables you to walk forward with strength and purpose, rather than weakness and lack of awareness, as you navigate your life toward the future.

The cards contained in this spread will never mislead you from the truth about your life and those who play important roles in it. This designation allows you the opportunity to prepare yourself for sudden, emotionally-charged shifts perceived to radically alter your path to the future in terms of your relationships. To take calculated risks with your career so you can embrace success in days to come.

You can't lose when you allow this designation to guide you in your readings. The cards in this spread make it possible for you to dynamically define your own existence, making your life all the more worth the living as you tackle Life's inevitable ups and downs, thrusting yourself toward a better, happier future as a result of what you perceive and ultimately, come to experience in days to come.

Face Cards and Imagery

Many of those who undertake the study of Personal Prophesy seem to have difficulty understanding and interpreting face cards. And yet they are actually the simplest cards in the deck to perceive with skill and accuracy.

At the beginner's level, you learned to call face cards "people cards" and for very good reason. Those cards represent the various people who enter your life, in past, present and future terms. Some of these people have a profoundly meaningful effect on your life; others merely represent momentary bystanders or those who are just "passing through" your life, but their purpose for being in your reading still has a certain amount of significance. They all come through in your reading simply because your life path is perceived as having turned in their direction and they will potentially play major or minor roles in it.

Perceiving who everybody is in a reading becomes easy when you read your own cards daily. In the beginning of this course, the people cards most likely represented complete strangers to you, which is perfectly natural. But at this point in your training, you will have at least a vague idea who one or two of these people cards represent in your readings. Understanding the rest will come, I assure you, with time.

To help you better understand the imagery attached to face cards and the significance those in your life have in relation to your reading, here's a good example:

You imagined me, Deborah, earlier in this book. You developed an image of "me" in your mind. The Queen of Clubs in terms of the cards represents me and if you were to perceive me in your readings, you would have a pretty good image in your mind of who I was in the cards and why I was in that reading, because you perceived me as such.

But chances are, I am not the Queen of Clubs in your own readings.

This card would represent someone much more closely connected to your life, because the cards, when you read them, represent the realm of your life, which I am not realistically a part of. I am vaguely connected to your life for teaching you this method. But I am not actively participating in it.

A sister, friend, co-worker, neighbor, a female you are emotionally attached to, would come through in your reading as the Queen of Clubs. She would bear the personality traits of a Clubs people card in general: inventiveness, making things happen, an individual more focused on philosophy and intellectual pursuits and the good of humanity rather than emotional attachments and matters of the heart.

An individual who is represented by the Hearts people cards would be perceived as being emotionally grounded in the way they live their lives. Hearts face cards literally refer "to the heart" and they are wonderful caregivers, nurturers and healers.

Those represented by a Diamond face card are perceived as materialistic and somewhat unemotional by nature, individuals who can handle money and financial transactions well, mainly because they don't allow personal feelings to get in the way. They are phenomenal in business, handling stocks and bonds, real estate.

Those who are represented by a Spades face card are generally perceived as possessing personality traits that would define them as seekers of justice, information-gatherers, and logical thinkers, analysts. They tend to be perceived as rather "aloof" emotionally. They make outstanding lawyers and judges, police officers.

The best tip I can give you in better understanding face cards in your readings is that you simply allow the people in your life to be represented by that card which comes through as suiting them best intuitively. Do bear in mind that with the passing of time, people will come and go in your readings, just as they do in terms of actual life. You will find yourself continually perceiving new people being represented by the individual face cards as you follow your own life path.

To better identify the face cards in your readings, make wishes for knowledge about people you know extremely well and circumstances about their lives which you are already familiar with. Family members, very close friends. You should be able to identify and establish an intuitive connection with at least a few of the face cards this way.

Understanding the Prophesy of Face Cards

When a face card in your reading is seen bearing a card which, say, holds a negative intuitive message for you – for instance, if that card were the Four of Diamonds – it is advising you to be cautious in your dealings with this particular person in your life, because he or she is perceived to have *the potential* to be untrue toward you... a "back stabber".

It doesn't mean they are actually taking steps to defame or malign you. It only means the *potential exists* for them to do so. This prophesy allows you the opportunity to handle this individual carefully, to refrain from trusting him or her unadvisedly, in essence, to protect yourself from emotional harm where they are concerned.

If this is an individual you have already had difficult problems with, that Four of Diamonds would be letting you know that the situation has not improved between you despite what he or she may say to you, and it could very well intensify in a rather negative, destructive way in the future.

Possessing this perception gives you the opportunity to be aware of the thoughts and feelings of others, to prepare in advance for actions they are perceived to have the potential to take as you move toward the future.

On the other hand, when a face card is bearing an extremely positive card – for instance, the Six of Hearts – you would be able to perceive from this card that, in a time of turmoil, this individual is focused on working things out and thinking the very best of you, seeking to find an honorable resolution to the problem the two of you currently face together.

Should no difficulties exist between you, that six would just as readily advise you that this person thinks the world of you and is focused on the promise of a beautiful, bright future yet to be shared with you.

As you progress in your training, let the cards that the face cards in your readings bear tell you what you need to know intuitively. But remember, the prophesy of the cards they bear in your readings are the perceptions of these individuals *at the time* you conduct these readings and are as subject to change as your own personal perceptions are as you live from day to day.

Homework Practice

Conduct a regular reading for yourself. Look for two good examples of face cards bearing positive or negative cards, which you clearly understand within the context of your reading. Try to specify to yourself who your intuitive voice tells you is represented by these face cards in terms of your life. Analyze the prophecy you were able to receive from them.

Chapter Nine
Deeper Perceptions Involving Love Cards

As you become more skilled at reading cards by the Personal Prophesy method, it will become increasingly clear to you in your readings that most people don't know what they want when they unexpectedly find themselves standing on the threshold of a new romantic relationship.

While they may ideally yearn to be in a healthy, happy, committed relationship, realistically speaking, most have a tendency to manage budding relationships badly. They advance aggressively when they should be holding back. They misinterpret the motives of the other people involved. They recklessly trust emotions generated by the moment, rather than taking the time to assess the situation and make more appropriate choices for themselves.

As your perception of relationships deepens in this training, you will find that the cards are remarkably accurate in revealing the hidden emotions of potential partners who enter your life, their personal motivations for acting as they do, and perhaps most importantly, what impact the choices they make will have on your life.

Which brings us to the single most important lesson you will ever learn regarding prophesy with cards and your dealings with other people: **There is nothing you can do to change the way other people feel.**

Did you get that? It's so important that I'm going to say it again: There is nothing you can do to change the way other people feel. And I do mean 100 per cent of the time.

Emotions play a vital role in reading cards, particularly in matters pertaining to love. You must always bear in mind that the thoughts, desires, and inclinations of other people are as personal and worthy of defense to them as yours are to you. Your greatest success will come from accepting this fact and learning to operate around the lives others are choosing to live, rather than wasting precious time and effort in attempting to bring their emotions to the point of change.

It cannot be stressed enough how vital that acceptance is for living a happier life. Truth can be difficult to accept, particularly when the cards reveal to us how much – or how little – others actually care for us. If you pin your hopes and dreams to any relationship that clearly does not have the potential to become reality, you are literally choosing to be a miserable human being.

On the other hand, if you accept the prophecy the cards have to offer you in terms of these relationships, your love life will improve dramatically and you will become empowered with insight and knowledge. As a result, you will choose not to pursue or cling to a partner who your readings have pointed out, is clearly incapable of making you happy.

Sexual Attraction

As you've learned, the Seven of Clubs is the indicator in readings of the initial interest between the sexes. When it appears in the reading *before* a face card (to the immediate left of it), the Seven of Clubs indicates *your own* primal instincts of attraction and sexual desire. When it appears *after* a face card (to the immediate right of it), it indicates the drives of the man or woman represented by that face card.

The individual perceived in the cards as bearing the Seven of Clubs ("bearing" meaning that the placement of the Seven of Clubs appears after the face card representing that person in the spread) is not infatuated, in love or seeking any kind of lasting emotional fulfillment.

He or she is merely feeling attracted at that particular moment. It doesn't mean they will feel that way 24 hours from now. Therefore, the Seven of Clubs cannot be relied on to indicate consistency or permanence in relationships, and your personal symbolism of this card must reflect that temporary feeling of attraction in your readings.

Perceive the sexual force represented by the Seven of Clubs for what it is – the drive for gratification of desire – and you won't go wrong. I guarantee it. If you are interested in developing a meaningful relationship with the man or woman who bears the Seven of Clubs in your readings, use this force to your best advantage. Encourage the sexual interest, but don't act on it – not until you know intuitively that the relationship has developed on another level. By being mindful of your cards, you can learn a great deal about the nature of this relationship and what lies ahead, should you choose to pursue it.

You can shuffle the cards and make specific wishes for knowledge before you count them off and lay them down:

- Wish to know if he/she will grow to love you.
- Wish to know if he/she is interested in making you happy.
- Wish to know if you would be satisfied with the end result of this relationship (sexual or otherwise) with this particular individual.

By doing so, you will have some insight as to whether choosing to go forward with this relationship will be likely to make you happy, even as it is only just beginning. As I can vouch from experience, that kind of insight can be priceless.

When to Act On Sexual Attraction in New Relationships, When Not To Act – and Why

Let me say that in all the years I've spent intuitively perceiving the future from a deck of playing cards, I have seen very few sexual relationships in the cards actually begin on a level of true love. Most romantic relationships take shape on a level of sexual interest first.

With that in mind, let's consider how the cards perceive sexual attraction between the sexes. Over the years, I have discovered that most men tend to view their relationships with women on the sexual level initially, while most women are led emotionally in their attractions at this stage. The end result? Males tend to be misunderstood in their pursuit of sexual release, and women tend to feel misled by the pursuit – which is, intuitively speaking, an avoidable situation.

Sexual attraction should never be confused with emotion. Can the cards actually differentiate between physical drives and emotional needs in this way? Absolutely. With careful thought and action, the sexual force perceived in the cards can be put to excellent use in the early stages of these relationships. When you understand this force for exactly what it is – the drive for sexual gratification – you won't go wrong.

Frequently, people act too quickly on sexual interest, even when it has been perceived to be to their detriment to do so. In some instances, they will try to reap a future from it, and live to regret it. All sorts of these people have come back to me and groaned, "Why didn't you warn me?" That's the important lesson in Personal Prophesy. You have to listen to the message to make it work for you. In every one of these cases, the prophecy was there, but unfortunately, the message wasn't heeded.

How can you use sexual attraction as a productive tool in your own life as you look for love? First, don't immediately act on it. Give that attraction time to intensify. Too often, people allow themselves to leap into the moment, failing to realize that an easily satisfied sexual attraction will fade as it is only just beginning. I've seen countless potential love relationships in the cards crumble because the parties involved jumped at the first opportunity to satisfy sexual attraction and then found themselves with nothing left to lead them toward the future together. An attraction that is not immediately satisfied can grow stronger, making it possible for a more meaningful relationship to develop in the meantime.

Here is a good intuitive guideline to follow as you meet new potential partners. When you feel that sexual attraction and don't act on it, and the individual you are attracted to loses interest and no longer pursues you, this is an important sign that he is not the right partner for you in terms of the future.

Sexual encounters rarely foster love. It's what occurs between two people before sexual gratification takes place that brings meaning and substance to the relationship. I see sexual attraction in the cards as a sword that cuts two ways. It can be used to your best advantage to inspire a relationship of substance (or conversely, to let you know that such a relationship is not a possibility), or it can be used against you, causing you to act injudiciously when it really wasn't what you wanted to do at all. Accept this attraction for what it is: the drive for sexual gratification. It is a powerful, self-satisfying force – and you will have no illusions about its prophesy.

True Compatibility

If there was ever a card to signify compatibility, the Six of Hearts would be that card. When a member of the opposite sex appears in your readings "bearing" the Six of Hearts, this is a positive road sign on your path to happiness. The Six of Hearts is the indicator of honorable pursuits and the realization of long-cherished dreams and wishes in love. It indicates the opportunity to enjoy genuine intimacy with that individual, the kind of intimacy, emotionally and sexually that leads toward courtship and the bond of marriage.

You can rely on the Six of Hearts to tell you that this relationship is beginning on the very best footing possible and its potential for the future is extremely powerful. Because of that message, the Six of Hearts draws us in its prophesy toward honor between partners and a solid commitment to common goals. When it comes to perceiving good marriages in the cards, I have found that they are first and foremost indicated by the Six of Hearts.

Where the Seven of Clubs cannot be relied on for stability and continuity, the Six of Hearts holds the potential for that to become reality, as well as promising to grow into something better and stronger far into the future.

The Six of Hearts, then, is a card of compatibility and promise. It offers new beginnings, the chance to make love happen. If a relationship with a serious future is one of your goals, the Six of Hearts will surely tell you when you have found it.

For an existing relationship, the Six of Hearts means a great deal. It indicates the opportunity for emotional growth and a period of tremendous enjoyment and contentment; the kind of satisfaction that brings people closer and fosters new intimacy for both partners as they proceed toward the future.

By its very nature, the Six of Hearts thrives on commitment and seeks it, almost to the exclusion of all else. It is certainly a card that promises love in its truest, purest form.

You can make specific wishes for knowledge concerning this relationship:

- Wish to know what the future holds for this relationship.
- Wish to know if your experiences in this relationship would make you happy.
- Wish to know if this individual will make a commitment to you.

By doing so, you will receive intuitive information about this relationship as it develops in the cards, so that if you decide to make it a reality for yourself as it presents itself to you, you will be guided toward making the best possible choices for yourself in the future.

Platonic Love

Platonic love – love that is spiritual rather than sexual and emotionally involved, is the deepest manifestation of friendship and is perceivable in the cards as one of the very best ways to share life with another person.

Some of the most beautiful relationships I have ever seen have been characterized by platonic love. It is the indicator of cherished, selfless bonds between people that are characterized by the desire to give rather than to receive, the eagerness to simply enjoy life experiences together without confinement or commitment.

You won't ever find platonic love associated with possessive or oppressive relationships of any kind. Nor, strangely enough, will you find it associated much with marriage, even those that are perceived as being "good" marriages. The love of freedom that is so inherent to the nature of platonic love is essentially incomprehensible in terms of marriage. Platonic love is about caring and caring very deeply, but it doesn't commit to someone in the traditional sense – it has no need to.

Platonic love represents a spiritual love. It isn't involved with the emotional plane. This kind of love has an intellectual quality that isn't interested in serving pledges or defining limitations, which probably accounts for a good part of the reason that so many friendships become troubled and eventually disintegrate, and so few are able to remain free enough to survive.

Genuine platonic love thrives on that sense of freedom in terms of equality and individuality. There is no control exerted over the relationship by either partner. Both are free to act as independently as they wish, without any threat to the security of the relationship. It is a strong, consistently mutual give-and-take association that is so meaningful and satisfying for both partners that it transcends all restrictions, including those imposed by time and distance, making it possible for people to maintain close relationships over great distances and for a long period of time, indefinitely, even with separations and loss of contact.

Some people refer to these harmonious friendships as possessing a rare "chemistry" that works for both people. Whatever word or phrase you choose, the prophesy in your reading of platonic love reflects that important spiritual quality of selflessness and freedom.

Platonic love doesn't appear in readings anywhere near as often as you might expect. Just as genuinely loving and loyal friends are difficult to find, the perception of platonic love in a reading, except under the most extraordinary circumstances (when a person is so blessed as to have an abundance of good friends, for example), is equally as rare.

Most relationships will be translated in the cards as being acquaintances (which, realistically speaking, most basically are), and only those that have the potential for achieving those bonds of selfless platonic love or have the potential for doing so, will be interpreted as such.

This is a fact you can rely on. Personal Prophesy will always point the way toward genuine friendship and, ultimately, let you know who your friends are. If you have been deceived or disappointed by those you confided in and depended on as good friends in the past, that trust need not ever be misplaced again, as long as you listen to the message of the cards and choose your friends accordingly.

I have seen countless numbers of clients who unconsciously manage their beautiful, platonic relationships as if they were miniature marriages, seeking unity through conformity and confinement and unspoken demands... *"As long as you perform or behave in the manner that suits me, we will continue to have an intimate exchange of friendship"* ... All the while these clients intensely fear change, when change and the freedom to be individual are actually quintessential to the future success of these relationships.

I had the experience to give intuitive readings for two women who had been extremely close friends, virtually for life. They were in their mid-twenties and had enjoyed a deep relationship from the day they met in kindergarten. Pattie and Mary kept no secrets from one another and shared practically everything. From their very first readings, it was evident that they shared those selfless bonds of platonic love, they had both found that "one true friend in a lifetime". The degree of compassion and understanding between Pattie and Mary was almost overwhelming. They couldn't have been closer, short of sharing the same body.

Over the months, however, a situation began to develop within the cards that indicated a real threat to this beautiful relationship and its future. A romantic relationship had recently ended for Mary with a man she had cared for quite some time. She was having difficulty accepting that the cards held no potential for the marriage she had been hoping for – in fact, there was no potential for reconciliation. What the cards did hold, however, was the plain truth about this man's hidden motives for ending his relationship with Mary in the first place. He was actually in love with Pattie, and he would go to great lengths to try and marry her!

The jealousy perceived as developing in the weeks ahead on Mary's part and the secrecy Pattie would find herself living with to spare Mary's feelings, had the power to totally undermine the strength of this friendship, because in effect, Pattie and Mary were already married – to being loyal to each other. Pattie was not really free to act independently of Mary because she had always been committed to sparing Mary's feelings over and above making herself happy. And from Mary's point of view, as long as Pattie lived up to her expectations, because she herself happened to be so good at resisting change, the relationship would always remain intact.

From the perspective of the cards, what they had actually managed to do very successfully over time was enjoy the security of a relationship that had never once been tested by conflict. And yet, here they were, fast approaching a point of critical change, where Mary's ex-boyfriend had the clear potential of becoming Pattie's husband if she chose for him to be – but at what cost? At the expense of the friendship between them that had been built over two decades? Or the illusion of permanence they had both found so much security in for so long?

By perceiving this situation in advance and accepting the prophesy of the cards as they did, Pattie and Mary were able to effectively prepare in the present for events perceived as becoming reality in the future. When Mary's ex-boyfriend began to pursue Pattie a short time later, their awareness of the situation made it possible for them to save a relationship that had previously been perceived as being lost, by altering that future consciously through choice.

After a long and painful process, Mary and Pattie were able to deal with the changes in their relationship and to actually work toward a stronger one in the end, regardless of what might ultimately occur between Pattie and Mary's ex-boyfriend. That is the power of platonic love.

If only all relationships could work out this way. Too many never do. Again, this is the one condition attached to Personal Prophesy: You have to listen to the message the cards offer you in order to make the prophesy in them work for you. When you do, you have the ability to change the future for yourself and reap considerable personal happiness from it –it's a choice that is yours to freely make.

Unconditional Love

The Ten of Hearts signifies the ultimate form of Love. It indicates the opportunity for redemption and rebirth through the most powerful experience of loving. While the Six of Hearts promises love, the Ten of Hearts simply gives it from the deepest, selfless reaches of the heart and soul.

This individual, intuitively speaking, seeks to forgive, endure and ultimately, overcome any hardship life may put in the path of his or her relationship with you, because the love they feel is so complete, so all-encompassing.

Your interpretation of the Ten of Hearts must contain the message of unconditional, perfect love in your readings as it relates to human experience: True happiness, the unity between oneself and one's ideals, the joy of beginning again or "being saved" through the bonds of love.

For those who have endured a period of severe loneliness or personal despair, the Ten of Hearts is a healing sunrise over darkness in terms of its prophesy; it indicates an end to suffering and a future perceived as filled with joy through the bonds of total commitment.

A relationship characterized by the Ten of Hearts holds the potential for a serious, long-term commitment, which will most likely culminate in marriage. When you see this card in your readings, it is letting you know this individual loves you from the deepest part of his or her heart and they will stand by you unconditionally. You have the ability to overcome every obstacle, which may come your way when the Ten of Hearts appears in the cards to protectively, and powerfully guide you toward the future.

You can get specific wishes for knowledge on this relationship as you see it developing in the cards:

- Will he/she truly love you.
- Will the two of you remain committed far into the future.
- Will you be able to make this individual happy with the passing of time?

By doing so, you have the opportunity to gain an accurate perception regarding the depth of this potential relationship and that insight will prevent you from making ineffective choices in terms of your own life and its future path toward happiness.

Romantic Love in Readings

There is nothing more beautiful to perceive in the cards than romantic love. It characterizes the realization of long-cherished dreams and desires. It also indicates an opportunity for commitment, in the sort of genuine intimacy that leads toward the bond of marriage.

The most important word you can associate with love perceived in its initial stage, traditionally referred to as courtship, is promise. The potential clearly exists for expectations to be met and satisfaction to be gained from things wished for on a deeply personal and meaningful level where love is concerned.

The individual perceived in your readings as "courting" you is someone who holds you in very high esteem, someone who truly admires and respects you, suffering your disappointments and failures with you, who cares tremendously about you. Many rewards can be gained from a relationship with someone who is perceived from the reading in this way. I have seen an overwhelming number of long-term relationships and marriages result from this sort of courtship, which is always evident in readings quite early on.

Courtship indicates that the relationship will begin on the very best footing possible and that "the sky's the limit" as far as the future is concerned. Love is an extremely powerful force in terms of its potential, in the present and most certainly, in the future.

For those people I have read for who have endured a period of severe loneliness or despair, the essence of this prophesy is like a sunrise over darkness, because it indicates an end to personal suffering and all sorts of wonderful new opportunities for happiness coming in the future.

It is wise to bear in mind, however, that the nature of courtship is idealistic, rather than realistic. It represents the highest of aspirations, the concept of things as they should be, the chance to dream and attain some of those dreams that have always been closest to the heart. The love perceived in courtship doesn't necessarily view people and situations as they truly are. In fact, courtship in its purest form refuses to accept limitations, which probably accounts for its ability to make the extraordinary happen.

Your interpretation of courtship must contain these "visionary" aspects, but this quality should never be confused with illusion or imagination in your readings. The intrinsic message of courtship is not "deception" in any sense whatsoever, but rather, "perfection" as it relates to human experience. It is happiness, the unity between one's self and one's ideals. It is the exhilaration from spiritually "beginning again" through love.

Because of that message, courtship represents honor between partners and a joint commitment to common goals. It represents the joy in having found a true soul mate. If you are looking for compatibility, *the prophesy* of courtship will bring it to you every time. When it comes to perceiving exceptionally good marriages in the cards, I have always found that they are first and foremost perceivable through courtship.

A case in point is the 1986 engagement of the famous late-night talk show host, Johnny Carson. At a time when he strenuously insisted to the public that he would not ever marry again, a reading of the cards "by proxy" – meaning that it was done without his presence or knowledge, a technique that works very successfully with the proper concentration – revealed that he was moving swiftly toward marriage in the autumn of 1986 and would soon announce his engagement to the woman he'd been dating. That's exactly what transpired a few months later. How was such a prediction possible? From the prophesy of courtship in Johnny Carson's reading, it was indicated that he was well on the road to "beginning again" through the bonds of total commitment and love for this woman.

Count on the prophesy of courtship to be an excellent guide to lead you toward people and situations that offer the most in terms of personal fulfillment.

Courtship, then, is the prophesy of compatibility and promise. It offers new beginnings, the chance to make important dreams come true. If a relationship with a future is one of your goals, courtship, love, will help you find it. Once you've achieved that goal, however, you wouldn't want to impose too much too soon upon the potential of this relationship. Courtship is only the seedling of the relationship that has yet to be. Put too much pressure on it or make too many demands of this fragile beginning, and, chances are, it won't survive. When you perceive a relationship such as this developing in your readings, be aware that while it holds strong potential for you, it's still tentative in its early stages and still subject to the effects of outside influences.

For an existing marriage or long-term relationship, courtship indicates the opportunity for emotional growth and a period of tremendous enjoyment and contentment. This kind of satisfaction brings people closer and fosters new intimacy. Courtship thrives on commitment and promises eternal love in its truest, purest form.

Keeping Love Alive

Intuitively speaking, keeping love alive, when so much of the outside world threatens to overwhelm it, is one of the most difficult challenges we will ever face in our lifetimes.

You might be thinking, "*Well, how in the world can that be? If you're really in love with each other, keeping love alive between you shouldn't be a hard thing to do at all.*"

I wish I could say this is true, but unfortunately, in terms of the number of years I have spent intuitively perceiving romantic relationships in the cards, falling in love is relatively easy, but keeping love alive is, realistically, one of the hardest things we will ever do.

Consider for a moment those beautiful, wondrous first days of being "in love". Everything about the experience seems practically perfect. You find yourselves meshing in ways you never thought possible. Your hopes and dreams seem so compatible it's as if you were born to be together. You feel such ecstasy and find such completeness in that loving, passionate embrace you share that you are convinced you have finally found "the one".

The question is, will that feeling of being "in love" last? From my experience with the cards, the answer is no, not unless you are willing to put a tremendous amount of time and energy into it. Being "in love" is that virginal, untried first step involved in loving. It's basically an overwhelming desire between two people to simply be together.

Love, real love, changes and grows as we ourselves do all the time. Every single day it requires tending and nurturing and only with time does it become strong and resilient. This is the love that develops into a bond between two people, and it has the power to carry them into the future together and at times survives what may seem to be nearly insurmountable odds.

When we are in love, what we feel is presented in the cards as if it were a young, innocent child. It needs a tremendous amount of protection and guidance as it matures and moves toward the future. Without that protection and guidance, this "child", this love, simply flounders, having no idea where it should go.

In reality, far too many of us are so "in love" with the love we feel for each other that we rarely, if ever, stop to consider the hardships we may inevitably face as couples in the future. For instance, there may be career changes, and financial problems. There is the stress of raising children. Then there are conflicts with relatives, illness or addictions, and outside temptations.

What we fail to realize is that the experience of falling "in love" is only a first step toward truly loving. It's the hardships and challenges the future brings and how we successfully overcome them, that actually brings depth and substance to the love we feel. Unfortunately, many of us are so in love with "being in love" that we never give ourselves the chance to advance beyond that first step.

Take a good, hard look at the divorce rate among us these days. Nearly 50 per cent of all marriages today end in divorce. Why? Simply because couples can't keep their love alive. One thing or another manages somehow to draw these couples apart. Perhaps there are too many problems, or maybe there is too much boredom. Sometimes too much personal growth on the part of one spouse and not enough on the part of the other can be the cause. And yet, I can't imagine many people marry expecting to get divorced.

Divorce is perceived in the cards as an unnatural breakdown in the process of loving. It means one, or both, of the partners involved has somehow allowed him or herself to lose focus in the relationship: they've lost faith, and they're essentially looking beyond the commitment in that relationship to achieve personal happiness for themselves.

On the intuitive level, commitment is perceived as a conscious agreement between partners to be together. But the bond that exists between them is something that runs far deeper. When two people are not truly "bonded" to each other, which takes a considerable amount of time and effort by both partners to achieve, it doesn't matter how "committed" they may outwardly profess to be. Their relationship is essentially doomed, intuitively speaking, practically from its beginning. Without that strong, solid emotional bond between them, keeping love alive will be impossible.

How do we achieve such a bond? For one thing, we wake up every day and see our relationships as genuinely living, growing things, and we care for them accordingly. We realize that being "in love" is an initial experience of passion and attraction, and we strive to build a much more meaningful foundation of hope and trust on both with the passing of time.

We exercise a tremendous amount of understanding and forgiveness in our relationships. With the right care and handling, today will become a more enriched, fulfilling tomorrow if we have been able to love unconditionally.

We do everything we can to stay "in love" by continuing to be the individuals we were at the start of these relationships. In other words, she still makes an effort to dress up for him when they go out to dinner. He still serves breakfast in bed for her the way he used to do when they were engaged. They continue to romance each other and be attentive to each other's needs, even when the dishes aren't done or the lawn hasn't been mowed. They essentially look for ways in the midst of everyday living to celebrate their love for one another, to literally keep their love for one another alive.

This may not be all the time, of course, but enough of the time. Often enough, to let partners know that even when times are troubled or if circumstances aren't quite what we'd like them to be, we are still very much "in love" in spirit.

You can keep love alive in your relationships, but it's up to you and your partner to make it happen. Plainly speaking, there is nothing effortless about love. In fact, genuinely loving our partners can be one of the toughest commitments we ever make in life. But the rewards to be reaped are enormous when we are sincerely committed to investing enough time and effort, enough of ourselves, into developing a loving bond that can truly last a lifetime.

Can You Make Someone Fall In Love With You?

Yes you can. With insight, ingenuity, and enough restraint, you can truly make someone fall in love with you, but *only* if he or she doing has the potential for loving you to begin with.

But, as much as we may want to, we can never make the wrong partners right for us. You could literally stand on your head to try to make someone fall in love with you, but if that person is not already inclined to take that "fall", it will never happen. This is where wishful thinking so often plays a major role in readings. We can get so caught up in our own hopes and dreams for the future that we tend to forget that the recipient of our love may just not feel the way we do. These people are, for all practical purposes, the sum total of their own life experiences, and what they feel or don't feel is as worthy of defense for them as our own feelings are for us. Still, we continue to persist. We send letters, make phone calls, and try to be in the same places they are, hoping that by persevering in our mission to have them fall in love with us, these people will inevitably succumb to our desires.

I'm sorry, but reality just doesn't work that way.

When you first meet someone, or you even just see someone at a distance to whom you feel attracted, the attraction doesn't necessarily go both ways. You must remember, that person is operating with a mind set that is the result of personal experiences within the framework of his or her own life. You can think you are the man or woman of someone's dreams, but unless this individual also feels this way, and unless an emotional connection between the two of you already has the potential for becoming reality, that connection will never take place.

I can't stress enough how important this realization is for finding happiness in new relationships.

From the outset we have people with entirely different points of view on life searching to relate to each other on some sort of common ground. That common ground will often initially take the shape of physical attraction, and if there is potential, that attraction will inevitably develop into a meaningful, emotional bond.

When you meet men, ladies, you need to remember: These men are initially being guided by sexual instinct. When you men meet ladies, you need to remember that they are operating from an entirely different value system from yours initially, one that begins and ends with emotion.

How do you find that common ground on which to build a strong, meaningful relationship in the future? To begin with, you can get an insightful reading from a good reader who will tell you if a relationship does, in fact, have the potential for becoming reality before you even attempt to spin your wheels. You can strive to establish a sound friendship between the two of you first.

We frequently dismiss friendship as not even close to being related to romantic love. Yet, friendship is the best foundation for marriage and permanent, loving relationships there is. You can allow the recipient of your feelings to take the lead in good time, while waiting and watching for signs that will let you know that they are interested. But no matter how hard you may try, you cannot force someone into feeling something for you if the potential is simply not there for him or her to ultimately feel it.

The future, whether we like it or not, comes in its own time and in its own way, and no amount of pressure or effort on your part will ever change that fact. Too often, when we meet someone where there is potential for a meaningful relationship to take shape, we try to make it happen for us immediately.

Relationships, good relationships, take time to develop and grow. They simply can't be rushed. If you were planting seeds in a garden, would you say, "I want to see fully ripened tomatoes here by tomorrow?" No. You'd tend that garden faithfully content to watch those tomatoes grow naturally, day after day. You'd care for them; watch over them with patience and concern, allowing nature to follow its own course. This is how we should view our relationships: as seeds in a garden that need our time, and attention, and patience as they slowly take root and grow. Rome wasn't built in a day and neither are solid, secure relationships that can withstand the test of time.

So how can you make someone fall in love with you when the potential exists for them doing so?

First, be receptive. Let someone you've met sit and talk about whatever happens to be on his or her mind, even if it's about pain from a previous relationship. Feeling secure enough to be able to confide in you is a big initial step toward establishing future intimacy.

Second, be a challenge. Nobody wants to pursue a meaningful relationship with someone who comes across as available to anyone who happens to look his or her way. Be challenging psychologically, intellectually and sexually. Let them know that you have a good mind, a caring heart, and the self-respect to share yourself sexually only with someone you love. Help them to feel that giving your time and attention, and later your affection, makes them, in your eyes, very special indeed.

Third, be forgiving. We've all been places and done things that we regret and are ashamed of. Forgiveness is the key to truly loving anyone in life. Whether it is a mother, father, lover, friend, or a child, forgiveness is the essence of true love.

Perhaps it is most important to allow the person you feel affection for the freedom to reach that important moment of caring for you by giving them time to reach this conclusion on his/her own. We are all, each of us, following our own individual paths toward the future and not necessarily operating from the same emotional levels. It can take time for someone to come up to speed emotionally. Be prepared to give that kind of time.

When a relationship has the potential for becoming reality, you will know it on a highly intuitive level. You will feel pulled, as if by an imaginary string, toward that person. You will feel a sense of completeness just by being physically near to them. This is the feeling that tells us, "I'm going to marry him or her one day." It is a feeling on a far, far deeper level than sexual attraction – even if you've only just met.

Love is a bond that can be readily intuited in readings. I've conducted such readings long before a relationship has ever been realized and long before two people have even met.

Once perceived, you are able to intuitively *know* when you have met that individual capable of making you fall in love, for real. You experience that feeling of "completeness." Your heart is suddenly made whole. Honest, genuine, lasting love isn't something you simply "fall into." It is something you just "know."

Chapter Ten
Dealing with Change and Difficult Cards

At this point, undoubtedly you are discovering that when you lay the cards down for a reading, they essentially present you with a puzzle, or perhaps more accurately, a complex riddle, which only you can solve. You may look at the cards in the layout and think, "The cards are trying to tell me something... the question is, what is their message?"

When you find yourself faced with such a dilemma, this is a clear indication, intuitively speaking, that your life is literally poised on the threshold of Change, important change which may prove to be so sweeping and dynamic in nature that the cards you see may not even appear to be "your cards" anymore.

Please have faith, when such a situation occurs, that those are in fact "your" cards. They are simply signaling you that Change is on the horizon, should you continue to follow the current path you are taking into the future. Remember, you hold the power to alter your life, in both major and minor ways, every single minute. If you are dating someone that you perceive in the cards is a relationship heading strongly toward the potential for marriage, you are the one who chooses to make that marriage a reality by allowing your life to continue in that direction.

If you were to decide to, say, become a nun or priest tomorrow, the future you've perceived for that relationship would, quite naturally, change, as a result of the new choice you've made. You would find yourself heading down an entirely new path in terms of the future.

If the cards indicate that conditions around your job are deteriorating as you experience growing difficulties and worry about your work, it isn't that job security and satisfaction are crumbling simply to bring hard times your way, the message is that the future is calling and attempting to bring you to the point of change.

You could choose to stay in your present position and do your best to make the best of a less-than-fulfilling situation until things get so bad – or your boss chooses to fire you – that you are literally forced to reach the point of change as the result of outside influences. Or, you could choose to perceive disintegrating circumstances surrounding your work as a sign that you have learned all you can from this experience and the time for change is at hand – change you can control, to a certain degree, by exercising productive choice in moving on with your career to a more fulfilling environment – choice which essentially propels you toward a happier, more satisfying future.

Choice isn't a magic wand you may think you hold in your hand; it is more like a divining rod which, with the intuitive messages the cards have to offer you, guides you toward a happier, more fulfilling existence.

Change is never an easy undertaking. When your cards present you with the prophesy of sweeping, dramatic change, the prospect can seem downright frightening. If you look at your life in terms of the bigger picture, you inevitably realize that change is the very essence of Life. As we live and grow, we are changing. Our lives are constantly in a state of change as a result. Nothing, ever, remains the same. Not relationships, work environments, our own viewpoints on life.

What we must do as our lives undergo these constant changes is hold fast to hope – hope that, as we endure the ups and downs that life presents us with on our own individual life paths, we are always moving toward that better tomorrow.

Perceiving Difficult Cards in Readings

As you have discovered, a number of the cards are easy to understand in terms of their prophesy: The Ace of Diamonds, the Five of Spades, the Ace of Hearts, the Five of Clubs.

A number of the cards, however, are not so easy to fully grasp within the context of a reading. You may find yourself feeling quite perplexed when you see these cards in your readings and quite possibly look at them, thinking, "What in the world are you trying to tell me?"

The following should help you better understand some of these difficult cards:

Four of Hearts, Spades, Diamonds, and Clubs:

The Fours represent crisis cards in your readings, particularly when they fall together in a spread. They indicate that you are potentially facing an unexpected, emotional crisis for yourself (or the recipient of your reading), where what has been a reality in terms of the past and presents holds the potential not to be reality in the future.

The Fours in the deck are indicators of abrupt change and urge you to prepare yourself for an approaching emotional setback. Unplanned experience is taking shape and is imminently on its way into your life. The prophesy (the message you receive) may be that a cherished loved one has betrayed you, knowledge that an unexpected chain of events will develop bringing disaster, or personal harm to yourself or someone, or that close illness or depression will overtake you.

The cards urge you to prepare for this unexpected experience which, spiritually speaking, is not intended merely to cause you pain, but to lead you toward a higher understanding of yourself and life as it is being lived by you and those around you.

Nobody likes seeing the Fours in readings. Unfortunately, they are cards that herald negative experience in order for us to achieve deep, inner emotional and spiritual growth. Whenever we encounter an emotional crisis on our life path, its primary purpose is not to hurt us, but rather, to help us grow. So do prepare when you see these cards in your readings. Their message to you is crucial and should never be ignored.

Nine of Diamonds:

Whenever this card appears in your readings, pay careful attention to it. This card is offering you important information about a situation or circumstance, which is currently affecting your life. While the Nine of Diamonds literally means indecision, uncertainty and in some instances, chaos, the prophecy attached to this card actually runs much deeper. When it falls in a spread pertaining to a certain relationship, this card is letting you know that you are either unsure about this particular person or he or she is feeling unsure about you (depending on who "bears" the card in your reading). This prophecy is an important road sign in terms of the future. Its message of uncertainty and indecision is most likely to be due to emotions still attached to a relationship in the past, which have not been fully resolved as yet.

People who are perceived as "certain" in the cards, move with purpose toward the future. Those who are perceived as "uncertain" in the cards are still being affected by the past on some personal level and are essentially hesitating where the future is concerned. You must move slowly and cautiously in this instance, until these people reach a point of emotional change within their own lives and become more "certain" about the future.

When the Nine of Diamonds appears in spreads relating to career or other intellectual pursuits, its message is that more work needs to be done, more effort must be directed toward making success in this endeavor possible. Make constructive changes in your current plan of action, and the Nine of Diamonds will disappear from your readings.

Eight of Clubs:

People often mistake this card, the indicator of "frustration", to mean that they must try harder in order to make something happen in their lives. Whether it's to get promoted, marry a certain individual, or simply feel happier about themselves, that misinterpreted definition for this card couldn't be farther from the truth when you see the Eight of Clubs in your readings.

A frustrated situation will only become more "frustrated" if you keep pushing to change it. You cannot make something happen if it does not already hold the potential, at that time for becoming reality, no matter how hard you may try.

The true prophesy attached to the Eight of Clubs is "back off", "give this situation more time to develop", in essence, "stop pushing to reach a place which is unreachable at this time".

You can learn a lot from this card when it appears in your readings. If you are tired of waiting for that "situation to develop", you can choose to alter the direction of your life by moving on toward something new and that prophesy of frustration will disappear from the cards.

You can choose to exercise more patience and by doing so, learn more about your own nature to be in too much of a hurry to achieve quick results. Sometimes the future requires a considerable amount of time before we get where we want to go.

This card reveals to us the true gravity of a situation or circumstance by perceiving the frustrated environment attached to it. Perceive its message correctly and you will find your life heading in the direction it is meant to go.

Seven, Eight and Nine of Spades:

You know these cards. They are the indicators of loss, tears and grief. Their prophecy is, essentially, deep, intense emotional pain.

We all have a tendency to view life as this beautiful, primrose-lined path we are supposed to skip along where only good things will happen to us along the way. When something tragic and emotionally devastating occurs, we think, "Why did this have to happen to me?"

Life is actually a rough and rocky road we all must endure which is only occasionally interspersed with stretches of happiness and pleasure. We just don't always realize this fact about life as we are busy living it. These cards literally challenge you in your readings to grow on all levels through pain by experiencing it, suffering it, and ultimately, overcoming it, as you travel your life path toward the future.

Some of us dwell on pain – or we do everything we possibly can to deny it – and fail to achieve emotional and spiritual growth as a result of it. Some of us wear such heavy cement overcoats all our lives that we never even have the chance to experience joy, let alone the pain, which is naturally attached to life.

Rest assured that when these cards present themselves in your readings, they are not offering you only the prophesy of pain, although it may seem that way when you first view them. They are offering you the opportunity to achieve greater wisdom, understanding and a far deeper sense of inner emotional and spiritual strength as you strive to overcome pain.

These cards are the ones which literally make the joy we experience in our lives that much more meaningful and rewarding. As a result, they make life that much more worth the living.

Choice and Change As Intuitive Tools

Now that you have developed a certain degree of skill reading the cards by the method you've been taught, it's time to start putting Personal Prophesy principles to use as you conduct your readings.

In this lesson, you will achieve a deeper intuitive understanding of how the **acceptance of change** and the **utilization of choice** profoundly affect the sequence of events in our lives, before these events have even occurred.

We'll begin by examining actual events that unfolded for an individual who perceived the prophesy of the cards as an opportunity for constructive change and effective decision-making, in contrast to another individual who did not. (The names of these individuals have been changed to ensure confidentiality.)

As you read these accounts, consider which cards you feel would best represent these changes and opportunities to alter the future in advance for these individuals, which will help guide you in your own readings to better utilize your own intuitive tools of choice and change.

Acting on Change

John Newman approached me for a reading at a time in his life when he did not expect to experience any dramatic changes, personally or professionally.

John was a 26-year-old radio announcer working for a small AM radio station in the Midwest. Even though he worked for an AM radio station and not the vastly more popular and contemporary FM, he felt secure professionally. He had earned considerable seniority at the station. His superiors, he felt, recognized that he was their most talented and listened to on-air personality.

While John did not believe he was facing any monumental changes in his life at the time of his reading, the cards, however, revealed otherwise. It was clearly indicated, as I conducted his reading, that within the next few months, John would experience a tremendous upheaval in his career due to a sudden and undisclosed change in the station's executive command. A male co-worker, who was seen in the cards as being radically shrewd and extremely deceitful, someone John absolutely did not like nor trust, was about to be promoted to a position above John. This man was perceived as having very strong intentions of seeing to it, out of petty jealousy, that John was fired.

John knew the identity of this particular co-worker when his reading was conducted and acknowledged that this man was in line for a promotion. Because there were so many tensions between himself and this co-worker, he had often considered looking for another job, but he'd always held back, afraid to take such a drastic step toward the future.

It was perceivable in the cards that John was extremely talented in his chosen profession but was basically wasting him talents. He had the potential to achieve enormous success in the broadcasting field by accepting change and asserting himself toward opportunity but he had to either choose to leave that radio station or be forced out, one way or another, to actually achieve that success. The cards conveyed to John that if he actively sought a job elsewhere in the country, he would quickly receive a firm offer from a station regarding a position that would be especially attractive in terms of salary and creative benefits, and represented a major advancement in his career as well.

John was single at the time. The cards indicated that if he chose to accept a new position and relocated, a romantic relationship would present itself almost immediately, offering John the opportunity to marry before the end of the year.

John had two options. He could:

1. Remain with the situation of the present and essentially do nothing (but remember, if you do nothing, you are basically allowing the choices of others to control your life). Conflicts at the station, however, were perceived as intensifying in the months ahead, eventually culminating with John's untimely dismissal.

or

2. He could accept the prophesy of the cards, viewing the situation as an opportunity to effectively deal with change and exercise control over his own personal destiny. He could, therefore, decide to actively seek that other job.

John had always toyed with the possibility of promoting himself to bigger and better stations in other areas of the country. Because the cards were a confirmation to him of his personal desires and offered a positive outcome, he decided to begin sending resumes and demo tapes of himself to other stations, "just to see what would happen." John received a call from one of the out-of-state FM stations that he'd applied to. He was flown in for an interview and pitched a very lucrative offer that was impossible to turn down.

Because he chose to act seven years ago rather than merely react where his personal destiny was concerned, he is one of the most listened-to radio announcers in the Midwest and is happily married to someone he met in that state. John heard the message (to accept the opportunity for effective change in his career) and he chose to act on it, voluntarily shaping his own destiny.

For some people, listening to the message of the cards and acting on that message, can be an extremely difficult, if not impossible, thing to do – as this second example illustrates.

Refusing to Act

Laura Johnson was a member of the Armed Forces Reserve. At the time of her reading, she was dealing with the trauma of having been abducted and raped by a superior while attending training in another part of the country. She was facing a court trial over the charges she had filed during this time.

Laura knew it wasn't going to be an easy case to win. There was no solid evidence and no eyewitnesses to substantiate her allegations. It was basically a situation of the word of the accused against her own.

She was, however, extremely confident that she would prevail in court, once all facts were brought to the jury's attention. After all, her record was exemplary and she had done nothing wrong, an attitude shared by her attorney, who assured her she didn't have a thing in the world to worry about.

Initially, the cards supported this viewpoint. Even though the reading indicated that the man accused intended to lie under oath and that these lies would seem very persuasive to the jury, the potential was still very strong that Laura would win her case exactly as she expected.

In a later reading, however, the cards revealed that a critical situation regarding this trial was developing. The defense, it was now perceived, had discovered a small, but legally significant piece of information about Laura from their pre-trial investigation. Once raised in court, this information had the power to destroy Laura's potential for winning the case entirely, by creating a major flaw in her credibility.

It was clearly indicated that if she lost the case, Laura would suffer a serious emotional setback as a result, which would have dramatic repercussions on the other areas of her life.

At that particular point in time, Laura had several options. She could:

1. Make the decision to go over everything that was even remotely related to the case carefully with her attorney, in an effort to locate and effectively deal with the information before it could be used in court against her.

2. Decide to engage a more competent lawyer who would be more inclined to anticipate such surprises in the courtroom.
3. Drop the case completely to void the risk of losing.
or
4. Basically do nothing.

Laura chose to do nothing. She was so convinced that her case, as it stood, was capable of convicting the man of the crime that she did not accept the message of the cards: that a serious oversight had occurred, requiring aggressive action in order for effective change of future events to be initiated. Because she did not take action, Laura lost her case in court.

Just as indicated in her reading, the defense disclosed damning information about Laura during the trial, proving that a small, seemingly inconsequential piece of information on her enlistment papers had been falsified. This single piece of evidence, compounded by false testimony on the part of the accused (which, the cards had already perceived in advance as swaying the jury), placed such sufficient doubt in the minds of that jury that her attacker was acquitted of all charges.

Do you see how the **acceptance of change** and the **utilization of choice** can, as in these examples, profoundly affect sequences of events, before they've even occurred?

John could have chosen to do nothing and left his future in the hands of other people, as so many do, all the time. He could have remained announcing on the local level until he was fired or, at best, managed to placate a miserable situation in order to salvage his career, sacrificing success and happiness just to resist change. Yet, when you really think about it, all he would have accomplished was an exchange of one sequence of events for another that was much less effective, logically leading to a whole new set of ineffective experiences.

There is no guarantee, of course, that Laura would have won her case in court had she chosen to act rather than simply do nothing, but she would have had a far better potential for winning had she accepted the message of the cards as the interpretation of the future as it realistically appeared before her and not merely wishfully thinking the future was locked in to meet her expectations.

Then, effectively acting on that awareness with a viable course of action would have ensured that no such surprises in the courtroom had the power to destroy her case completely.

In one way or another, we all tend to cling to our illusions of permanence, allowing ourselves to feel comfortable with a false sense of security about a future we know nothing about. We tell ourselves that "wishing will make it so", and are willing to go to all sorts of lengths to restrict ourselves, simply to resist the effects of change. By learning to live life more intuitively, the future becomes a moment in time that is of our own creation, and we can overcome our fears in order to live happily in that moment.

Are you a John or a Laura?

In terms of Personal Prophesy philosophy, we are all, realistically speaking, one or the other.

If you are a "John", you accept the message of the cards as an opportunity to effectively utilize the tools of Choice and Change within the framework of your own life. You perceive the future while living in the present, making a conscious choice to do what you can to change that future for the better. By doing so, you *voluntarily* shape your own destiny.

If you are a "Laura", you hear the message of the cards but refuse to heed that message, instead relying whole-heartedly on chance and the choices others are making around you, which inevitably puts you at the mercy of their choices and causes your own personal destiny to be shaped *involuntarily*.

When you lay the cards down for a reading, remember: The cards are reflecting the course you are currently following into the future. Those cards are offering you extremely valuable messages that you can choose or refuse to accept as you move toward the future.

If you are a "John", you will put those intuitive messages to good use by making constructive changes which will help guide you toward a happier, more fulfilling future. If you are a "Laura", you will do nothing, allowing the future to bring all sorts of unexpected and sometimes, unhappy surprises to you.

Choice and change are tools that belong to you intuitively. Use them to your best advantage. They are the very foundation of Personal Prophesy.

Homework Practice

Read the section about John's reading carefully. What cards may have been in his reading and why? Read the section again about Laura's reading. What cards could have guided her in this reading, in your opinion, which she chose not to act on?

Chapter Eleven
Altering the Future
Using Personal Prophesy

No doubt you are beginning to experience a comfortable familiarity with the cards, as well as a growing awareness about each card, in terms of its uniquely personal message for you.

Your own **interpretation** of each of the cards in the deck is beginning to not only take shape in your readings but also take over, where the literal meanings you were initially given left off.

In other words, it is an excellent sign, when you place the cards in a layout, to hear a voice inside you say, "This card doesn't just mean _____, it also indicates _____."

That "voice" is your own intuition speaking to you. The more you listen to that voice, the more it will offer to teach you about the cards, individually and collectively.

This is the point where you begin to enter uncharted territory in terms of your own personal readings and the readings you will conduct for others. You'll put to use the fundamentals you have learned about Personal Prophesy, but the largest portion of your journey into self-discovery begins right here.

Visualize that, up to this point, you have been traveling a well-plowed road in winter, and now you've encountered a wide expanse of beautiful, untrampled snow, which stretches endlessly before you. The snow is not deep and invites you to begin making your own personal path into it.

The path you make for yourself into that snow may circle and wind, take turns here and there, drive straight ahead – it is, after all, a path which belongs to no one but you. Remember, you have the freedom to make that path as the intuitive voice inside of you guides you to make it. This voice can only guide you most accurately when you spend enough time with your cards, listening to the messages that voice from within has to share with you in every layout.

Potential for Reality

One of your most important tools for properly interpreting the future in your readings is a clear understanding of the Personal Prophesy phrase, "Potential for Reality."

We all know what reality is. It is the state of something being *real*. The fact that you are alive is reality. You work, you may have children, you may have bills to pay. This is reality. Being engaged to be married, mourning the death of a loved one, feeling happy at this precise moment, these are considered to be realities.

Wishing to be a successful actor or a multi-millionaire at this particular moment in your life is "reality" in the sense that you may be really wishing for such success, but the possibility – the *potential* – for this sort of success to take shape in your life and become "reality" has yet to be determined by the path your life is currently taking into the future.

Potential in your readings will always indicate an event or a state of mind, which has the capability to develop into actuality (in other words, "reality") based on your life path at that particular time. Potential does not mean that what you are perceiving will necessarily become reality, only that it has the necessary ingredients to quite possibly *become* reality, under the right circumstances. This is a deep concept one that you will come to understand fully, in time.

Remember John? His cards indicated a productive career move had the potential for becoming reality in terms of a better job at a radio station in another part of the country as appeared to be indicated in his reading. The right ingredients for that event taking shape in the future were clearly perceived in his cards and he felt inclined to act on that prophecy.

Laura's reading showed that winning her court case did *not* have the potential for becoming reality based on the action she had taken to that point. Yet, had she viewed the lack of potential in her reading as a viable avenue for change, her cards would have indicated a dramatic change in her court case in terms of potential.

Let's say that you feel romantically attracted to someone you've just met. You go home and wish on the cards, "Will so-and-so feel the same about me as we get to know each other?" What you receive for information in response to that wish is that he/she faces someone else. You see a strong love card attached, or perhaps an emotional card indicating loss involving a partner from the past.

This would indicate that at least, for the present, this individual is emotionally focused on someone else and until he or she decides to shift that focus, there would be no potential for the two of you becoming romantically involved.

Now, of course, you could still choose to pursue a romantic relationship with this individual despite the message of the cards, but chances are remote that such a relationship would occur at that point in time.

What if the cards held a positive message about that someone you just met? Then, yes of course, the two of you becoming romantically involved in the future did have the potential for becoming reality and you would be well advised to pursue that future relationship.

Let your cards be your guide in matters involving "potential for reality." They won't steer you wrong when you do. But when they tell you, "This does not have the potential for becoming reality," and you try to push the future to go the way you want it to go, you will undoubtedly find that you would have been a lot happier listening to the prophesy your cards had to offer you first and acting, second.

Does **potential for reality** change within the context of readings? Quite often, it does. The lives other people are living change from day to day as ours do. Their ways of thinking and the choices they make all change as well.

We are always changing, always becoming, essentially, always evolving into someone "new" as we move toward the future. What may not have had potential for becoming reality three months ago could be perceived quite differently in the cards today. It's how we choose to act on that "potential" when we see it and perhaps more importantly when we *don't* see it in our readings that can mean all the difference in the world between merely attempting to live happier lives and actually achieving the happiness we seek.

As you repeatedly shuffle the cards and lay them down for readings, you will find yourself constantly learning something new about the placement of the cards in these readings, as well as the more intricate meanings of the cards themselves, both individually and collectively.

Chances are that you are beginning to achieve a personal awareness within yourself of subtleties and meaningful details about the cards that you are slowly, intuitively teaching yourself.

You will continue to increase your own personal, intuitive knowledge as you read the cards and may find yourself reading them in a way which may not be the same as anyone else. Bear in mind that you are following your own personal course toward intuitive self-discovery, which doesn't have a thing to do with the course others are taking as they follow their own life paths into the future.

Now, we will study more about the philosophy behind Personal Prophesy by focusing on an example reading for Gloria, a woman currently separated from her husband. She has been married before and has children. Let's assume she came to you for this reading and shared with you, before you conducted this reading that her life is very difficult at present, but she is trying to do her best to cope. As you begin her reading, you can clearly see that her life is in a state of serious transformation, that she is undergoing the *evolution of emotion.*

Evolution of Emotion

Human emotion, in terms of the Personal Prophesy philosophy, is a complex subject. Emotions come in all shapes and varieties. There are those that we find ourselves experiencing right now as we live in "the moment," those we have experienced for quite some time, and those we are only just beginning to feel as we move toward the future.

Most people don't realize there is an "evolution" attached to the emotions they feel. They aren't aware that what they feel today isn't necessarily how they will feel tomorrow or in the many tomorrows yet to come. People tend to want to live and express their emotions in a steady, unchangeable world. This just isn't possible when you consider that our lives are, and always will be, in a constant state of flux.

I often suggest to those I conduct intuitive readings for to try to imagine themselves standing in a wind tunnel in terms of the lives they are living. I ask them to envision the future as the wind blustering toward them, and the past is the wind wafting behind them. When you are able to view your life in this fashion, you realize that the "you" standing in this wind tunnel experiencing the inconstancy of the present, is significantly influenced by the change the "winds" of the future brings your way nearly every minute.

Our emotions are the same, compelled by the past to thrive, and yet they are driven by the future to change. It's how we deal with them in the present that makes all the difference in the world. Emotions, whether you are aware of it or not, are always in a state of change. They are either becoming stronger, or they are disintegrating, becoming entirely different emotions as we live our lives.

Consider, two people who have enjoyed what they always perceived to be a happy, loving, and committed relationship for a substantial amount of time. Suddenly, in the midst of all that happiness, they find themselves reaching a critical point of conflict. Regardless of the circumstances involved (yes, even including infidelity or another serious breach of faith), this couple breaks up. He goes his way, and she goes hers. She's hurt and he's angry, or vice versa. They have chosen to take separate paths toward the future, but their emotions will quite naturally undergo change in the process as well.

With the passage of time, he will undoubtedly find himself becoming less angry. He will either choose to spend this time on his own, or he will become involved with a new partner. As his emotions evolve, he will find himself thinking about and, inevitably, missing at some point in time that woman he loved and angrily left.

She may feel hurt and dwell on her pain for quite some time. She may even run from partner to partner, attempting to escape the pain she feels. But, in time, her own emotions will evolve to the point where perhaps she realizes she didn't want a new partner for herself at all.

Time, and the experience of being apart, eventually holds the power to bring this man and woman back together. A whole new level of understanding has occurred where their emotions are concerned. Their emotions have evolved to the point where they are ready to embark on a positive, new beginning, together.

When we first experience an emotion like love, it is an emotion still very much in its infancy. We are awed and overwhelmed by the experience. It is a beautiful, new feeling in our lives. We tend to view life as if we were looking through newborn eyes, and, as a result, we are caught up reveling in the splendor of the moment. Then we begin to gravitate toward commitment. We feel so captivated, so sure this is the partner we want for the future, that we idealistically consume our time making plans and sharing the dreams, hopes, and wishes that seem to harmonize quite naturally with those of our beloved.

Once we become settled and feel secure in that commitment, reality begins to set in. We find ourselves having disagreements, engaging in arguments, and perhaps evaluating the worth of the relationship as a result of those disputes. Emotion is obviously evolving within the context of that relationship.

Those in tune with their emotions will have a relatively easy time adjusting to the evolution their emotions undertake. They have gained the wisdom and enough foresight to know that relationships don't exist in a vacuum and that change is an essential part of life. They will put in a great effort to keep a relationship thriving, in the midst of change.

Those who aren't in tune with their emotions might shield themselves with the comfort of denial: "I'll just pretend these problems aren't happening and they will go away." Or they may run from the relationship entirely. But the evolution of their emotions will inevitably make them realize that while they can run, they will never be able to hide from the truth their own hearts speak to them.

As you engage in loving relationships, the best piece of advice I can offer you is to always be prepared for change. It will occur, whether you are consciously ready for it or not. Your relationships are evolving even as you are reading these words, and that evolution can be your best friend or your worst foe, depending on how adaptable you are in terms of your relationships.

If you have a partner who you believe truly loves you allow that partner enough space in which to grow and change emotionally. Realize that today is not yesterday in terms of your relationship, and that you are both striving in your own way toward a satisfying love-filled tomorrow.

If you are enduring the aftermath of a painful break-up or coping with one about to occur, remember: what that partner leaving you feels today won't be the same emotions he or she feels in the days yet to come. Try your best to let this partner go with the knowledge that you love him or her and only want the best for this person in the end. By doing so, you leave an important door open. This individual may walk through this door once his or her emotions have evolved to the point where it is realized how much you mean and how much this person yearns to share the future with you.

Conducting Gloria's Reading

As she cuts the cards, her wish is to reconcile with her husband. She is not actively dating at this time. When you arrange the cards, the **Nine of Hearts** is present. If the Nine appears in the first layout for a reading, it indicates that the answer at the time the reading is being conducted is rather clear-cut, one way or the other. If it takes a second or a third layout to get the Nine to appear, it means the answer to the wish is still hazy or somewhat "distant" in terms of the reading. If you do not get the Nine in three layouts on the same wish, this would indicate that the future has not shaped enough as yet to provide an answer. It can also indicate that the wish itself does not hold the potential to ever become reality.

On the top row you see: **Eight of Diamonds, Eight of Spades, Ten of Clubs**. These three cards, loosely speaking, represent "current atmosphere" of her life in general.

Reading these three cards together, my perception would be that the **Eight of Diamonds** represents her existing relationship with her husband. The **Eight of Spades** would indicate tears, sadness, and the **Ten of Clubs**, a legal document (divorce papers). I would perceive this to mean, "He is moving toward divorcing her, because he has been so hurt in this marriage."

If, however, the **Eight of Spades** were a more positive card, for instance, the **Six of Hearts**, I would think, "He wants this divorce for reasons which are correct in terms of his life at present."

When you read the cards, you must try your best to perceive "why" particular cards are in a spread; in other words, what would motivate the individual to feel what the cards are expressing. This spread would tell me, in terms of Personal Prophesy philosophy, that this woman's husband still cares for her, but he is heading toward divorce because the pain he feels regarding this marriage is pushing him in that direction.

Moving to the first spread in the second row, these indicate Home and Matters Pertaining to Home. We find the **Jack of Spades, King of Spades**, and the **Ten of Hearts**.

The **King** is facing the **Ten of Hearts** and the **Jack** faces the **King**. My perception of this spread would be that this woman has an opportunity to date other men but because they are turned away from her, it would indicate to me that they would be more focused on fulfilling their own needs emotionally and would, therefore, not be that interested in fulfilling her own. I would advise her not to consider either as satisfying long-term mates for the future. Had they been facing her in this reading with the **Ten of Hearts** behind them, I would consider either to be good potential partners.

The next spread is "Matters Pertaining to Herself". This includes the **Queen of Spades, Queen of Hearts**, and the **Nine of Hearts** – her wish card.

Remember, her wish was to reconcile in the future with her husband. This spread would tell me that her husband's attention is focused on two other women at this time. I would then go directly to the spread designated as "Pertaining to Her Wish" in this reading, because no matter where the **Nine of Hearts** falls in a reading, this spread provides additional information, intuitively, about the wish itself.

In the Wish Spread, you find the **Four of Spades, Ace of Diamonds,** and the **Four of Hearts.** Ah, you think. The Four of Spades indicates this wife's feelings in regard to her marriage at this point (depression), but the **Ace of Diamonds** followed by the **Four of Hearts** indicates her husband and his current emotional state.

He is obviously, within the context of this reading, reacting out of jealous, hostile feelings about his marriage to this woman by concentrating his attentions on those two other women, but this spread tells us that he is not happy; he has not found closure at all. His emotions are still evolving at this point, and it is quite possible that after some time has passed, he will move on from this jealous, hostile emotional level toward either full resolution and healing where this marriage is concerned, or he will miss his wife and long for her, at some point in the future. For the present, however, he is still mired in these extremely negative emotions, which indicates that he has some distance to go before he might reconcile with his wife, but it is still within the realm of possibility.

Moving on, the next spread is designated as "The Unexpected" and holds the **Two of Spades, Ten of Spades,** and the **Queen of Diamonds.** These cards would tell me that this woman could quite likely find herself moving a great distance in the future to be closer to the light-complected woman who faces her in this spread. It doesn't mean it "will" happen, only that within the context of this reading, this move holds the potential to "possibly" occur in the future. And because there are no negative cards in this spread, it would be perceived as a positive change for this woman.

The next spread, designated as "The Expected" holds the **Jack of Clubs, Four of Clubs** and the **Five of Spades.** The Jack is turned away from this woman and focuses on his own misfortune and anger, as depicted by these cards.

I would perceive this spread in her reading as an intuitive warning to be cautious in her dealings with a man who would be represented by a Club, because were he to experience a personal setback in his life because of her actions, he would retaliate in a very angry fashion as a result. I would watch to see what role this particular man would play in subsequent readings. If he were to re-appear again and again, this would mean a situation with him is developing and will most likely take shape for her in the future. I would strongly advise her to be cautious of such a man.

The next spread in her reading designated as "Surprise Events" holds the **Eight of Clubs, Nine of Spades**, and the **Three of Spades**. My perception of this spread would be that she should try to guard against worrying and allowing herself to become extremely frustrated in the days ahead as she conducts her routine business, for such feelings could have a boomerang effect and make her feel that much more aggrieved about her life. Because I would have advised her of this, in terms of Personal Prophesy philosophy, she has the opportunity to change the future by knowing in advance that she needs to guard her state of mind.

The final spread in her reading, designated as "What is Sure to Come True" holds the cards, **Three of Diamonds, Six of Diamonds**, and the **Ace of Clubs**.

This spread would indicate to me strong potential for petty disagreements and conflicts to erupt between herself and her husband (the Six representing an existing relationship, which I would perceive within the context of this reading to indicate her relationship with her husband) during an upcoming phone call or possibly in written correspondence.

By making her aware of this potential, she has the ability to ensure that she remains composed in future communication with her husband and doesn't allow herself to be drawn into a petty quarrel with him.

Homework Practice

What would be your own personal summary of this reading had you conducted it for this particular woman? Don't worry about giving the "right" answer; instead focus on your own perception of it. In other words, what would be your overall advice for her at the conclusion of this reading?

Chapter Twelve
Sharpening Your Personal Prophesy Skills

You've learned enough about the "mechanics" involved in reading the cards by the Personal Prophesy method that you should now be able to perceive some intuitive prophesies or messages about the future from them, even though these prophesies may seem to be sketchy and rather vague to you at this point.

Chances are, the cards still haven't proven themselves to you to the extent where you implicitly trust them whenever you sit down to conduct a reading. That kind of trust and confidence only comes from time, experience reading, the cards and concentrating your efforts on expanding your own personal level of intuitive perception, which can be a very slow process at times.

You may even find yourself feeling quite confused when you view your cards and seriously struggle to determine what messages they are attempting to give you. That is also quite understandable at this point. When you lay the cards down for a reading, you might try thinking of yourself as a foreign exchange student who has learned the fundamentals of a language in a classroom and now must learn to communicate in that language on a day-to-day basis with the natives of the land you have traveled to.

Essentially, Personal Prophesy is a foreign land and you have embarked on a personal journey specifically designed to help you learn and understand the unique language which belongs to this foreign place. It comes with time and practice, the ability to understand and fluently communicate through this language. If you moved to a distant country and only had a simple understanding of the language, you would be patient with yourself and wholeheartedly focused in your effort to learn to communicate with people in this faraway place.

Allow yourself the same sort of patience as you learn Personal Prophesy and your own level of intuitive perception expands. Achieve that same sort of focus in your study of the cards and the challenges you face in processing intuitive information will steadily diminish.

In order to accurately "process" intuitive information, you must first be open and receptive to the opportunity to receive it. When you conduct a reading, try your best not to have pre-conceived notions about the cards as you are cutting them and laying them down. Simply lay the cards down and **then** take an objective, general overview of what you "see" in them.

Sample Scenarios

Suppose that your wish for knowledge in a particular reading was: "*I wish to know how "X feels about me.*"

Let's assume that "X" is an individual you happen to care for very much but you are not in a relationship with any more. Things ended badly between you and you are now seeking intuitive information from the cards about how this individual currently feels toward you. Let's assume the spread you receive intuitive information from looks like this:

2 of Diamonds   9 of Hearts   8 of Clubs

This spread would be telling you that "secretly" (**2 of Diamonds**) this individual is "frustrated" (**8 of Clubs**) about you. The **9 of Hearts** in this spread is, of course, your "wish determiner", alerting to you this prophesy about your wish. If you felt unresolved in your own heart about this past relationship, this spread is giving you some vital intuitive information about this individual you are no longer attached to. It is telling you that he or she feels "secretly frustrated."

Anybody who is intuitively perceived as "frustrated", as in this scenario, has not found closure yet. Even if he or she ended the relationship, they appear to still be coping with emotional aspects connected to it. They are not quite as "done" with this relationship as they had outwardly professed to be by ending it.

If they had found closure, if they were as "done" as they would have you believe, the cards would fall more like this:

Ace of Spades (apex up)   9 of Hearts   6 of Hearts

In this spread, you would readily see that the relationship in his or her heart was over (**Ace of Spades**) and that they were taking a bright, new, promising road into the future (**6 of Hearts**), unencumbered by the emotional effects of this past relationship.

This is where "processing intuitive information" comes in. Now that you have knowledge perceptually about this individual, you have the opportunity to work with that knowledge and bring about a "new future" for yourself and this relationship.

An individual perceived as "frustrated" may be receptive on some level to working things out, although it may take considerable effort, time and understanding on your part to get him or her there. Your cards are essentially telling you that this individual still cares, or they would not feel the frustration represented by the 8 of Clubs.

In this instance, you have the ability to deal with this frustration by being pleasant the next time you see them. Let's say you run into each other in a public place and you smile and say "Hi, how are you?" and you leave it at that. You'd be surprised how many times you'll later conduct a reading to find that "frustration" on the part of this individual has been replaced by remorse and longing in your cards because you had intuitive insight about their state of mind and worked with the prophesy you had received, rather than unadvisedly working against it.

In another scenario, let's assume that you have been asked by your boss to prepare an important report. This is a job you enjoy very much but perhaps don't receive much recognition for because you are not as well educated as the others on the staff. Your wish for knowledge in this case is, *"Will the boss be pleased with my report when it is finished?"* Let's say that you haven't begun the report yet, but want to gain some intuitive insight about it first.

The spread providing you with information about this wish looks like this:

6 of Diamonds   6 of Clubs   2 of Hearts

This spread would be telling you that a relationship exists (**6 of Diamonds**) where work or effort is the focus (**6 of Clubs**) which potentially leads to success and accomplishment (**2 of Hearts**).

This would be an encouraging intuitive message for you, that if you put in serious effort, you would receive a better return on this investment of "effort" than just a pat on the back. I would view such a spread in this context to mean a wonderful new door to the future has the potential to open as a result of the work done to prepare this report. In processing this intuitive information, you would find yourself thinking, "I could really get recognized for this report and be more in line for that promotion I've been hoping for." Because you received the message in the cards, you now have a new mind set to guide you, to put effort into that report, which you may not have done had you not had intuitive insight beforehand.

Now take a look at a more complex scenario. Assume that you are in a committed relationship and your life together is pleasant. Not particularly passionate, perhaps even humdrum in ways, but this relationship is essentially very comfortable and satisfies enough of your needs that you feel content to remain in it.

One day in a very casual way, you happen to meet someone, someone who seems to really mesh with you in terms of interests and personal philosophies. Someone who manages to set your hair on fire in the way that he/she thinks and feels. You become fast friends with this someone and begin to spend time talking and sharing, together.

When you conduct your reading and make this wish for knowledge, *"Why do I enjoy the company of this individual so much?"* And the cards pertaining to this wish come up as:

4 of Clubs   2 of Spades   10 of Hearts

The intuitive information offered by this spread would be difficult for anyone to accept while in a seemingly-content, committed relationship. This spread would be telling you that you are traveling a path in terms of this new friendship which spells misfortune for the future of the relationship you are currently in (4 of Clubs) as you grow and change as a result of your experiences with this new individual (2 of Spades). This new growth would be perceived to be bringing new love into your life (10 of Hearts) if you choose to continue to follow this path.

This is where the "choice and change" principles of Personal Prophesy come into play in your readings. The message these cards are sending you is, "Continue on this path and you will experience the decline of your current commitment as a new one takes shape within the framework of your life for the future." You have the option, as you process this intuitive information, to choose to follow this new path into the future. Misfortune as perceived by the 4 of Clubs would most likely develop into pain for your current partner and guilt on your part for having grown away from the life you've shared. But within the context of this scenario, the change of heart represented by the 2 of Spades is perceptually a very positive change in that you are about to be reborn, literally, through the bonds of sheer, complete, genuine love.

Now, of course, you could choose to remain with your current partner out of obligation or because this relationship is such a strong comfort zone for you, but you would inevitably find yourself struggling terribly to resist the powerful, driving force of real love intended to take you on a new spiritual journey into the future.

If you were to make such a choice, your cards would change and fall like this:

7 of Spades   9 of Spades   10 of Hearts

For a lengthy period of time, you would find yourself grieving the loss of love which was meant to be but never had the chance to become reality, because you chose to remain in your comfort zone rather than allowing yourself the opportunity to risk change and grow emotionally and spiritually.

Understanding the Intuitive Message of the Cards

If your perception of your own life has changed as a result of what you perceive from the cards as you learn to more accurately read them, I am sincerely happy for you. The path of personal spiritual and emotional growth is a lifelong journey and the cards will help you achieve a more meaningful life for yourself the more that you study and get to know them, the more that you spend your time laying them down and reading them.

If you find you are still struggling, don't despair. By continuing to concentrate and working hard to expand your level of intuitive perception, you will inevitably find your own life in the cards and gradually reach a deeper understanding, which will guide you far into the future.

The most difficult aspect to the whole experience of "reading the cards" is interpreting what you intuitively *feel* from them into actual language. Try not to concentrate at this point on finding the right words to express what you feel from the cards. Instead, simply allow yourself to "feel" the message and to comprehend that message intuitively, without searching for the right words to consciously define it just now. In time, you will find yourself doing both simultaneously: intuitively interpreting and consciously defining into words what you see in your card readings. Because this level of the course offers more complex aspects of Personal Prophesy to study and master, those who graduate from it will be well on their way to becoming true professionals in terms of this skill.

Consider that your intuitive mind, as you arrange the cards for a reading, has the ability to understand what you see on a highly complex, inner level. It processes this information on its own and helps to give shape to your own conscious thoughts as you move toward the future.

When you view a spread, your intuitive mind knows the content of the message contained in that spread without having to describe it into actual words to you. This is the part of you, which *perceives* the message.

Your conscious mind, on the other hand, has been taught to associate certain words with certain cards and speaks these messages in a conventional language to you: "This situation will be extremely painful to resolve," or "The outcome of this situation looks very hopeful," "More patience is required for what I wish to become reality". This is the part of you that *articulates* the message.

Allow the messages the cards offer you to *guide* you intuitively, rather than struggling to express in words what you see in your own readings.

When you are reading the cards for someone else, of course you'll need to use words and in time, you'll learn to simply let yourself "speak" so that the words *flow* out of you. Your intuitive mind will, through practice and training, eventually speak these words fluently for you.

Comprehending Complex Cards Intuitively

Chances are, you have come across a card or two in your study of Personal Prophesy, which has confused or baffled you along the way. Here are three that most people tend to have the most difficulty with:

1. The Nine of Hearts

The rule of thumb on the Wish Card is that if it does not appear in three separate layouts while asking the same question, the readings of these layouts are not null and void. The absence of the Wish Card only indicates that the answer to that wish is still too hazy or too far in the future to be properly ascertained one way or the other at this time. Circumstances surrounding this wish might be in a state of chaos. The party (or parties) involved may not feel motivated or emotionally interested in what you are specifically wishing on where they are concerned. You may be presenting your question to the cards in such a way that an answer is not possible. And sometimes, no answer is, in itself, the answer although we may not realize this as we attempt to intuitively interpret the cards at that particular time. In all of these instances, the cards are telling us to find another way to pose the question, which will help us to better understand a certain situation in more specific terms.

In reference to the **Nine of Hearts**, ask your question in a variety of ways and eventually it will appear in your readings. When it does, it is sure to offer you the information and insight you need.

2. The Face Cards

As you advance in your study of Personal Prophesy and develop stronger skills as a result of long-term practice and concentration, you will discover that the face cards in the deck are actually multi-dimensional. The King of Spades, for instance, can represent one particular male in your life or it can represent several men, depending on the other cards that are connected to it in a spread. The more you work with face cards, the more you will come to understand the subtle nuances associated with them, which will enable you to intuitively "know" that in one reading, the King of Spades represents your father (for instance), in other cases, a co-worker, or a lawyer.

When a spread contains nothing but face cards, this is also an important intuitive message. This spread indicates an accelerated social life or a widening social circle approaching for you. A spread of this nature heralds more social activity and contact with others. In a professional environment, it indicates more opportunity for networking.

3. The Two of Spades

The "change" represented by this card isn't nearly as permanent as newcomers tend to believe it to be. Yes, abrupt and decisive change is indicated when you see the **Two of Spades** in your readings. While it symbolizes all sorts of change: a change of course, change of emotion, change of plans, change of lifestyle, it quite often represents a fleeting, short-lived change.

Human beings are prone to change, if you think about it, particularly when it comes to the heart. Someone who has a change in feeling today can just as easily experience a change in feeling tomorrow. We learn from our own life experience, which often compels us to make choices (changes), which we come to realize later were not the best choices to make after all.

Therefore, try not to be rigid in your interpretation of change in your readings. Remember, we all make mistakes from time to time. The more you can bring this type of insight and understanding to your readings, the better your ability to accurately perceive the messages in the cards will be overall.

Frequently, newcomers say that the readings they conduct for themselves seem disjointed. Intuitive messages don't always make sense. They struggle to fluidly conduct a reading but find themselves stopping and starting at every turn.

As you practice and gain more experience reading the cards, the following guidelines may be helpful to you:

1. **View the layout in its entirety.** Which spreads immediately jump out at you as containing important information? Which spreads appear to contain only trivial information? By viewing the layout as a whole, you gain an initial impression of the atmosphere of the reading in general.

2. **Read the spreads from the top of the layout to bottom.** Which spreads have you seen in previous readings? You will find that the cards have a tendency to repeat themselves. These repeating spreads are meaningful in that they let you know certain situations have the potential for taking the shape of reality in your life the more frequently they appear in your readings.

3. **Remember that what you "see" in a particular reading** is the path your life is perceived to be following at that moment toward the future. It isn't a fixed, rigid course. You hold the power to alter that course by exercising your own individual free will. The cards are simply showing you the path you are traveling. They don't define that course with rock-solid predictions, ever. But if you choose to continue to follow that particular course, much of what you perceive will become reality as a result.

As you progress with your study of Personal Prophesy, you will find yourself developing certain personal practices or rituals which will enable you to feel more prepared or ready to initiate the task of shuffling, arranging and accurately reading the cards whenever you choose to sit down to do so.

I encourage these rituals as they invite your body, mind and spirit to become centered and fully focused on the act of accurately reading the cards. By training yourself to become oblivious to external noise and activity, as well as clearing your mind of your own casual, day-to-day thought processes, these personal rituals help you to properly prepare yourself to receive and accurately interpret the messages the cards hold and intuitively offer you. You may find yourself preferring a favorite chair or a room in your home to conduct your readings in. A preferred time of day, for instance, early mornings as you drink your first cup of coffee, or late evenings just prior to retiring for the night. You may light candles, play special music, and spend a few moments meditating. There is no prescribed formula for preparing yourself intuitively, this is something *you* develop and establish for yourself over time as you practice and study the principles of Personal Prophesy.

Concentrating on Hopes and Desires in Your Readings

For those times when you are conducting readings for yourself with a particular hope or desire in mind – for instance, to be reunited with someone you love, receiving an important promotion on the job, achieving a personal, cherished dream – and you perceive in the cards that this particular hope or desire has potential for becoming reality within your life, try the following visualization exercise. You might be pleasantly surprised at what occurs in the future as a result of it.

1. Mentally picture yourself as physically in that place or with that person you care for. Really put some effort into this. Close your eyes, see yourself there, actually *feel* yourself there.
2. Drawing in a deep, deep breath as you focus on this mental picture, visualize yourself suddenly raising up a hand which holds a

faceted gold bar, which you thrust very high toward the sky.

3. As you hold up that gold bar, visualize the sun's rays shining down and glinting on it in a beautiful prism-like effect, sending many shafts of golden light out into the world away from it.

4. Hold your breath as you visualize this, feeling the warmth, the energy of that golden light as it is emitted from this moment in time. You will soon experience a powerful sensation in your chest of completeness and unity, of literally being "one" with this moment.

5. Visualize yourself bringing the gold bar back down and clutching it very close to your heart as you slowly exhale. Experience the tremendous amount of purity and energy contained in that moment.

6. The more you repeat this visualization, the more familiar with it you will become, the more peace you will feel within yourself and the stronger the energy will be as it is emitted in that golden light.

Meditating on the Cards

Most likely you now have several favorite cards in the deck, which you are very happy to see when they present themselves in your readings. These cards are taking the shape of becoming your own Personal Cards, in that they hold significant personal messages and substantial intuitive meaning for you. They may be cards of promise, love, commitment, and hope, cards that offer you meaningful intuitive sign posts in your readings that you look for in your layouts and receive comfort or encouragement from whenever they appear.

When you are experiencing difficulty in your life, these cards can be meditated on. Put that particular card or cards in your pocket or purse, or tuck it under your pillow. Take these cards with you and focus on them during your day. Meditate on the message of that card and project yourself toward a happier future in your meditations. Allow your Personal Cards to offer you guidance and understanding as you struggle with difficult times. We all experience them; it's in how we manage them that we become all the wiser for these times and are able to achieve happier, more complete futures for ourselves in the end.

Homework

Which cards do you perceive to be your own Personal Cards and why? What particular practices or rituals do you observe before you conduct your readings? Focus your insights on achieving more accurate readings for yourself and the methods you have found to better facilitate readings, particularly during troubling times.

Chapter Thirteen
Technically Advancing Your Skills

At this point in your training and card reading practice sessions, no doubt you are discovering that the deck holds a vastly larger number of more significant cards in terms of feeling and interpretation than it does those that are less significant. Some of the less-significant cards may strike you as being quite trivial in their meanings and perhaps even cause you to question their purpose within the context of readings in general.

While I would never encourage disregarding the less significant cards when conducting intuitive readings, I would advise that these cards be given their proper weight within the reading as a whole. In other words, view as cards holding messages of typical, everyday activity and thought as your life moves forward from one experience to another.

Because our lives are not a day-to-day conglomeration of emotionally-charged experiences, we will often perceive days and even extended periods for ourselves in which these less significant cards seem to fill quite a bit of space in personal intuitive readings.

Whenever you find this is the case in your own readings, the interpretation you draw from these cards would most likely fall into one of the following categories:

1. Readings filled with less significant cards often indicate that you

are living your life on a level focused mainly on routine matters, a series of momentarily-fulfilling, yet emotionally-shallow activities and experiences. While this isn't necessarily a negative way to live, the prophesy if too many of these cards are surfacing in your readings when you do yearn to get more out of life, is to take assertive steps toward becoming more involved socially with others and more emotionally connected to those who enter your life in the future.

2. An excess of less significant cards in your readings when you feel you are living your life on a satisfying, emotionally fulfilling level is an intuitive confirmation for you that you are, in fact, truly happy and well-connected to those currently in your life.

Deciphering Significant Cards in Readings

Let's take a closer look at those cards which are considered to be Significant Cards in readings:

- **Face Cards:** Face cards in your readings are always monumentally significant. They represent individuals from the past, present and future, which, intuitively speaking, play or have played a role of importance in your life. Remember, the lives we are living today are emotionally and psychologically shaped by our experiences yesterday. People are crucial in terms of that experience.

- **Nine of Hearts:** Without your Wish Card leading the way, it would be difficult to ascertain an accurate, intuitive answer to questions posed to the cards in personal readings. As you become more experienced with the cards, you will find this card becoming more and more meaningful to you.

- **Two of Hearts:** Without question, a highly significant card. It indicates a prophesy of self-fulfillment, happiness and personal completion of goals and dreams, emotionally and spiritually. A card of guidance, it intuitively lets you know that you are on the right path and should continue to follow it toward the future.

- **Ten of Hearts:** Love in its truest, deepest, most unconditional expression. Forgiveness and strong healing are associated with a relationship. Genuine bonds of love are indicated by this card. Without it, a relationship flounders and struggles, yearning for the bond of true, unconditional love signified by this card.

- **Six of Hearts:** Promise and courtship (essentially meaning, commitment of spirit and the energy of hope combined) points the way to a happier future.

- **Seven of Hearts:** True, fulfilling, honest friendship. This card is a guiding, intuitive star in our platonic relationships with others. When it isn't present in your readings, guard against trusting and investing too much of yourself emotionally in those individuals who fail to be represented by this card.

- **Four of Hearts:** An extremely significant card in your readings. The jealous, devious, hostile nature of this card helps us better understand the often-hidden motivations of others in our associations with them. It prophesies their own weaknesses, lack of self-esteem, personal insecurities about themselves. This insight gives us considerable leverage in our dealings with individuals perceived to bear this card.

- **Three of Hearts:** Regret is a strong, significant indicator in readings. An individual perceived as regretful is a sincerely apologetic individual. The prophesy of this card is that a new start in a relationship can be achieved.

- **Ace of Spades:** You may perceive endings and new beginnings before they occur and to anticipate them, as a result of the appearance of the Ace in your readings. Distance and location can be ascertained, providing you with important insight regarding face cards.

- **Nine of Spades:** This card is deeply emotional and extremely personal. The experience of feeling and emotionally acknowledging grief is intuitively perceived as the first, crucial step toward healing. When present in your readings, the essence of this card is painful need, in that it motivates us to seek relief from the pain we feel and propels us toward the future to heal ourselves of it in the most constructive manner we can possibly find.

- **Eight of Spades:** This card indicates tears, sorrow and hurtful longing, which is not the same as the need interpreted in the Nine of Spades. "Need" indicates the urge for relief from pain and the drive to somehow alleviate ourselves of pain and drives us to move toward a future moment without pain.

"Longing" in the context of this card, however, contains a sense of continuing to dwell on that intense hurt experienced in the present moment. A person who sits down and sheds tears has yet to experience the "need" for relief from pain associated with the Nine of Spades. The moment they are caught in is one more of hurtful "longing". It doesn't indicate moving toward a better tomorrow, only that they are focusing on the expression of "tears and hurt" in the present.

- **Seven of Spades:** This card, representing "loss" in your readings, is tremendously significant in your perception of the past, present and future. It can encompass losses on the physical level as in the loss of a treasured belonging. It also represents loss on a more emotional level, as in the loss of the love of your life. This card indicates the personal "seeking" of that which has been lost. The bearer of this card will not rest until that loss has been resolved. It represents a tie to the past which cannot be broken as a result of this constant "seeking."

- **Five of Spades:** When you find this card in your readings, get prepared. Anger is perceived to drive and compel you – or the individual who bears this card – into expressing some extremely strong and difficult truths. The venting of such intense anger will either clear the air and put you on a better course toward the future, or cause a breakdown (at least momentarily) in a relationship linked with this card.

- **Two of Spades:** Change is the very essence of life and touches our lives in a variety of forms. This card represents sudden impulsive change, temporary change, permanent change. As you gain experience with the cards, you will intuitively know the type of change you are perceiving in your readings as a result of your own experience and level of intuitive knowledge.

- **Six of Spades:** This card is highly complex in terms of Personal

Prophesy readings. On the one hand, it indicates careful thought and the exercising of caution in our dealings with others. On the other hand, at times it can also represent pregnancy, birth and the raising of children. You will find, as you continue to study this method of intuitively reading cards, your own personal interpretations of such cards as this one, taking shape for you as you progress and gain experience reading the cards for yourself.

- **Four of Spades:** Be watchful, should this card present itself in your readings. This card prophesies a depressed, "ill" feeling in connection to your life or an important relationship you may share with someone else. Depression concerning a relationship is often related to a sense of personal disappointment and a feeling of "I'm not going to continue to be happy here unless things change." This is your opportunity to strive to make things better so that this card doesn't evolve into another card prophesying change of heart, commitment or direction, ultimately impacting your life for the future.

- **Ace of Diamonds:** A vastly significant card here. The essence of this card is strong, abiding Unity in terms of marriage, commitment, and beliefs. There is longevity associated with this card and an important sense of purpose.

- **Two of Diamonds:** Be wary of secrets or secretive activity. Straightforward, honest, above-board individuals would never involve themselves in any type of hidden, secretive behavior. When you find this card present in your readings, it's a warning sign to you that events are occurring behind the scenes, which you are unaware of. Be cautious and careful.

- **Four of Diamonds:** Any time you see this card present in your readings, be sure to have your guard up. This card is alerting you to serious trouble. You are either being lied to, misrepresented to others or on the receiving end of unfaithfulness by one close to you. It can also indicate that you will soon be faced with a situation where you will be dishonest toward others, depending on how the cards fall in a particular reading.

- **Nine of Diamonds:** This card is extremely significant in that it provides you with intuitive knowledge of uncertainty and indecision. You will come to know, as a result of the prophesy of this card, whether to move forward assertively or to hold back. This card, when perceived properly, will help you avoid making mistakes when circumstances are not yet settled around you.

- **Ace of Clubs:** This card, representing Communication, aids us in the decision-making process and brings new, important information our way, frequently, when we need it the most.
- **Four of Clubs:** When you see this card in your readings, be heedful of it. It is warning you of potential circumstances, which could bring setbacks your way. By paying attention to the warning message of this card, you have the ability to prepare yourself, to make wiser choices as a result of it, and often, to alter your path toward the future in such a way that you side-step the unexpected misfortune intuitively attributed to this card.
- **Three of Clubs:** I consider this card to be one of the best in the entire deck. A dynamic, powerful card which possesses the energy to bring productive change our way, alter our lives dramatically for the future, put our hopes and dreams closer into focus as the future takes shape and becomes reality right in front of us.
- **Five of Clubs:** This card, which signifies agreements and commitments, helps us complete our own life's goals. This card assures us that we are relying on the right people, contracts and circumstances, and making the right decisions for ourselves. This card expresses an intuitive message of strength, commitment and resilience. When you see it in your readings, you know that you are on the same wavelength and forming a meaningful commitment, which will be able to weather difficulties that should arise.

Establishing Deeper Intuitive Focus and Concentration

The following material is designed to take you deeper in terms of your knowledge and perception of the cards, so that your readings will contain a sharper clarity and stronger intuitive message for you when you sit down to conduct personal readings for yourself and others.

Thus far, you have concentrated on perceiving the "message" without really knowing how to actually apply these messages to your life. Because interpreting and applying these intuitive messages to our lives is a highly complex and extremely personal aspect in terms of actual perception, it can take years before we fully understand how to successfully accomplish this.

Please bear this in mind as you continue in your study of Personal Prophesy, what you understand intuitively at this point is not any-where near what you will achieve in terms of understanding Personal Prophesy in the many tomorrow's yet to come. Your perception is in its infant-stage at this point. With concentration and nurturing, es-sentially through continued practice with the cards, you will achieve great maturity in terms of your perception over time, finding yourself relying on your ability to perceive the future, while applying intuitive messages to your life more and more in the years ahead.

Personal Cards are those cards in the deck which hold personal messages of intuitive meaning for you. They may be cards of promise, love, commitment, hope, cards which offer you meaningful intuitive signposts in your readings which you look for in your layouts and are able to receive comfort or encouragement from whenever they appear.

Significant Cards are those cards in the deck which hold important intuitive information and bring emotional impact to your readings. These cards convey meaningful messages about individuals who figure in your life and provide essential insight into situations which comprise your life – cards intended to guide you from this moment in the present to more productive and fulfilling moments in the future.

In this lesson, we will concentrate on those cards in the deck which, when they fall in certain combinations, are considered to be Critical Cards in terms of the serious intuitive messages of warning they bring to readings. While at first, you may find most Critical Cards to be alarming in terms of their prophesy, bear in mind that the intuitive message of these cards is not to frighten or to cause you to feel apprehensive about experience perceived to have the potential for becoming reality in the future for you.

The true essence of these cards is to alert you and provide you with the awareness that steps need to be taken to either:

1. Do as much as you can to prevent a critical situation from taking shape which will impact and greatly influence your current path to the future; or
2. Allow you the time to prepare for an event which is perceived to be unavoidable as your life path leads you toward the future.

Do bear in mind that whenever Critical Cards appear in readings, simply possessing this intuitive information in advance will often be more than enough to direct your path away from such potentially life-altering setbacks for the future. The intuitive messages the cards offer you are based on the path your life is perceived to be taking at that moment. This path shifts and changes daily, if not hourly. Never ignore these cards in readings for yourself or for others. The potential contained in these warnings is extremely crucial to future happiness.

Certainly, heed the messages of the cards but by all means, don't become fixated on them. Critical cards simply warn us of potentially serious situations. They don't hold iron-clad guarantees that these situations will actually become reality within the framework of our lives. They do, however, offer us the opportunity to exercise some extremely important principles of Personal Prophesy.

This lesson will show you some examples of Critical Card Spreads in readings. For now, let's concentrate on four classic spreads containing Critical Cards which you will encounter from time to time in your readings:

Seven, Eight and Nine of Spades

These cards in a spread prophesise extreme grief and suffering; a potentially-threatening period of lengthy mourning for an individual. Visualize this spread as the longest, darkest road of despair that anyone could possibly take toward the future. There is no hope attached, no strength, no faith, just an utter and complete sense of emotional anguish and helplessness.

Remove these three cards from your deck and place them in a

spread in front of you. It doesn't matter in which order these cards fall in a spread. In any combination, the intuitive message is fundamentally the same.

When you find these particular cards in a spread in your readings, you must give them your full attention. This spread alerts you to a potentially threatening and possibly dangerous situation where your emotional health (or that of your reading recipient) is concerned.

If you discover these cards in a spread at a time when your life appears to be in perfect order, this spread is alerting you to the possibility that a distressing event could take shape and cause you to experience a profound sense of grief as you follow your path to your future. When you see these cards repeating themselves in your readings, this is a sign that you have not as yet steered your life path away from this event.

When this occurs, choose to work at emotionally preparing and strengthening yourself in advance rather than wasting energy on worrying over a situation which may not actually occur and consequently, impact your life. By choosing to do so, you significantly alter your path in terms of foresight. By choosing to exercise caution in your activities and daily affairs, assessing your life and reminding yourself that most personal growth for the future results from overcoming hardship in the present, you also significantly alter your path in terms of awareness.

When these cards appear in a spread of a reading at a time when you (or the recipient of a reading) are coping with an extreme amount of grief, they issue a warning that becoming completely engulfed with suffering will dramatically affect the future. This emotional engulfment, if left to intensify, makes productive decision-making nearly impossible. If steps aren't consciously taken to achieve a more positive viewpoint or professional help isn't sought as the condition becomes severe, deep depression and contemplation of suicide could swiftly result.

In these instances, it's vitally important to plant strong seeds of hope in yourself (or your reading recipient). By doing so, you intuitively process the message of these cards and actively choose to change their prophesy in terms of the future.

Life is never a truly hopeless proposition for any of us. The intuitive challenge, when we confront such a spread in readings, is to achieve a sense of hope for ourselves when our lives seem darkest and filled with an extreme amount of personal suffering.

Visualize hope as a tiny beam of light shining through our darkest hour; one which can surely guide the way, and us, out of such profound grief.

Fours in the Deck

Any two or three-card combination of the Fours in the deck which fall in a spread in a reading prophesies an unexpected crisis developing in your future with the potential to severely affect emotional, physical and spiritual health. Always heed the message of the Fours in your readings. When they come together in a spread, they are warning you of a sudden, serious setback on your path to happiness. Events are perceived to be taking shape which will bring unexpected upset and emotional upheaval.

You might visualize the crisis symbolized by the Fours in the deck whenever two or three of them happen to fall in a spread together as an instant, intense blurring of vision, as if you couldn't see straight suddenly due to an unforeseen event occurring which takes on crisis proportions right from the start.

Some examples are: The moment of discovery that a partner is having an affair, an argument at work which suddenly escalates into on-the-spot termination of employment, losing a case in court you thought for sure you would win. There are many other situations which the Fours will prophesise as a personal crisis in readings, of course. These cards are extremely individual in that what you may consider to hold crisis proportions for your life, based on your own values, perceptions and emotional strength. What may not be a crisis for me or someone else within the context of our own lives could easily be a crisis for you. Bear that fundamental difference in mind as you conduct your readings.

When you find these cards coming together in spreads in your readings, try to assume the point of view of your reading recipient and do your best to concentrate on emotional preparedness for an unexpected emotional crisis. All you really can do when such crises develop seemingly out of nowhere in readings is try not to lose your true focus in terms of the bigger picture as you prepare for these situations in advance of their potential occurrence.

A crisis is a critical point on your path to the future, yes, but inevitably that moment of crisis tends to pass fairly quickly. Your path to the future will shift naturally as a result of it. While coping with the aftermath of such an upsetting experience, in terms of Personal Prophesy philosophy, strive to understand that most critical events occur in our lives for an important spiritual reason.

As you process the experience, the more you choose to grow from it, the more you are presented with the dynamic opportunity to achieve new strength for yourself, find deeper wisdom about your life and ultimately, point yourself in the direction of a new, more meaningful future.

Because the Fours in the deck impart such crucial intuitive messages in Personal Prophesy readings, let's break them down into more specific detail here:

Four of Diamonds: Visualize the intensity of this card as act of cheating, untrueness or backstabbing. This person does not care that the act will cause you excruciating pain. If anything, they want to hurt you and have every intention of doing so, whether it's with lies, hateful acts, or unfaithfulness in your relationship with them. Always see this card as a warning to keep your guard up and trust nothing about the situation you are perceiving from a particular spread in your reading which contains this card.

Four of Hearts: Visualize a person you love, how that person loves you. Really feel that love. Now, visualize a third party coming along, perhaps a very close friend, who approaches your partner and does everything within his/her power to lure your partner away without any regard or respect for your relationship. Concentrate on how hurt you would feel in such a situation. Where the Four of Diamonds is essentially a cold-blooded act of untrueness, the Four of Hearts is a card of intense envy, greed and even outright hatred. This card represents a yearning for revenge, retaliation, the opportunity to take something precious triumphantly from someone. It's a very anguished, needy card that can naturally fester itself into obsession quite quickly.

If you find the two red fours next to each other in a spread, you must be very cautious. Their coupling means the feelings attached to both are doubly intensified.

Four of Spades: You know how you feel when you've got a virus or you wake up one day and life just looks and feels dark? That is the essence of the Four of Spades. It literally means depression and illness, but think of it in terms of that "I'm-coming-down-with-something" feeling. What you could be coming down with is a gloomy outlook on life but this card will warn you that you have physical illness coming on, too. If it were connected to the Four of Hearts, the message would be a strong one.

Four of Clubs: Literally this card means "misfortune." In readings, I see it as a shattered window. One minute the glass was intact and you were looking through it, out at the world, the next minute, the glass is shattered – crash! – and so much for that beautiful, serene view on life. The Four of Clubs warns of unexpected accidents, ranging from a simple mishap to a life-threatening situation. As you learn, you will get a better feel of this card, achieving your own interpretation for "misfortune" as it appears in your readings.

Ace of Spades (apex up), Two of Spades and Nine of Spades

In a spread, in the above order these cards prophesies that you are facing an abrupt critical point of change in your path which will inevitably cause great pain in the process, but will also offer you the opportunity to grow emotionally and spiritually as this experience potentially takes shape for the future.

Consider the weight of these cards by placing them in a spread as described above. It should be clear to you in looking at them that an individual could easily come to dwell on the grief prophesied by this combination. If you are, however, someone who has the determination and inner strength to confront the emotional hardship that change is indicated to bring your way, you will practice the Personal Prophesy principle of choice and change.

By choosing to strive to overcome the grief represented by the Nine of Spades and view this potential situation as a door abruptly closing in terms of your life, there will also be one just as quickly opening to a more fulfilling future, once you have processed your grief and resolved yourself completely of it.

Four of Clubs, Ace of Hearts and Ace of Diamonds

These cards in a spread as given above, urge you to reconsider the choices you are making for yourself which are perceived to profoundly affect your home and marriage in a most negative way. To proceed on the path you are following to the future is prophesies from this spread to radically harm that secure, safe, loving place in which you dwell.

Should you continue to follow this path, the cards in this spread indicate that you would inevitably come to re-affirm your own personal commitment to your home and marriage in the end. We must always remember, however, that because we have learned from our own mistakes in making wrong choices for ourselves, it doesn't necessarily mean that those who share our lives have participated in the same learning process right along with us.

Many times in readings, I perceive spouses who have made regrettable mistakes within the context of their commitment to marriage – choosing the wrong friends, engaging in affairs, not rising to the defense of a partner during heated disputes with relatives, etc. They were perceived to be truly sorry for their actions and yearned to re-affirm their commitment from the deepest part of their hearts, only to find that their marriages and homes had been emotionally compromised by such a serious mistake in judgment in the end.

Just as we proverbially "can't go home again", it's an intuitive certainty in readings that once we have taken a step in the wrong direction where our commitment to marriage and family is concerned, trying to take that step back to be in the place we used to stand in is, while not impossible, is extremely difficult and tends not to happen successfully in the long run.

As Personal Prophesy teaches us, it's vitally important to always weigh choices carefully before we act on them, particularly those choices which will greatly impact in the process what essentially matters most to us. Even though we may later wish with sincere earnestness to re-affirm our commitments to those we love after we've made a serious mistake, we may come to find that such a mistake has dramatically altered our path to happiness where our loved ones are concerned.

Homework

It's Quiz time – time for you to show me how well-developed your own personal perception of the cards has become, particularly in reference to Critical Cards.

The following are three-card spreads containing two or more cards considered to be Critical in readings. Read each three-card spread and explain your own interpretation of these spreads. Describe what steps you would take emotionally and spiritually to guide yourself in terms of the messages involved, if you were to find these spreads in your own personal readings.

Bear in mind there are no right or wrong answers here. This quiz is designed to help you better understand the messages contained in your own readings in general and your readings for others, which you will learn to conduct in future lessons of this level. Arrange the following combinations into spreads using your own deck of cards.

1. Ace of Diamonds + Four of Diamonds + Four of Clubs =
2. Nine of Spades + Seven of Spades + Ace of Clubs =
3. Your Face Card + Two of Spades + Four of Hearts =
4. Four of Spades + Four of Clubs + Ace of Spades (apex up) =
5. Four of Diamonds + Four of Spades + Ten of Hearts =
6. Eight of Spades + Four of Clubs + Four of Diamonds =

7. Four of Diamonds + Four of Clubs + Four of Spades =

8. Seven of Spades + Face Card + Ace of Spades (apex up) =

9. Your Face Card + Four of Diamonds + Four of Four of Hearts =

10. Ace of Diamonds + Four of Diamonds + Seven of Spades =

Chapter Fourteen
Preparing For an Important Intuitive Breakthrough

That's right! You are swiftly approaching an important intuitive breakthrough in your study of Personal Prophesy. Through the end of this instruction, what you learn will bring a whole new dimension to your readings and your ability to not only perceive the future but in many instances, alter it in ways you might not even imagine are possible. First, let's concentrate on more technical information.

In the study of Personal Prophesy, newcomers tend to consider the word "critical" to indicate only unfavorable, serious, perhaps even dangerous situations – several of which were outlined in the last lesson. In many readings, this will in fact be the case.

Critical Cards, however, can also contain a far more positive and empowering message – particularly those cards which indicate an approaching powerful, rejuvenating turning point. These cards in readings represent rocket ships to the stars in terms of how profoundly thrust forward an individual's life can be in terms of happiness, success and fulfillment.

Described here are those Critical cards considered to contain positive, intuitive messages.

Critical Cards Containing Positive Messages

- **The Tens:** Whenever you find three Tens sitting in a spread together, you are viewing an extremely dynamic set of cards. Even when the rest of the layout appears terribly dark and negative in content, three Tens in a spread are advising you that a major shift in your life path for the better is on the horizon, a shift you will rejoice in and celebrate, far into the future.

  It doesn't matter which of the suits the three Tens are appearing from, or even their particular order in the spread. Three Tens in a spread are sending a vitally important message: "Prepare yourself – a powerful new way of life is about to unfold for you."

  You will often find three Tens in your readings when you feel you are at the end of your rope, when current circumstances seem so overwhelming and practically insurmountable that you can't imagine yourself ever being able to see your way through the extreme difficulties you face. Out of the blue, there they will be, those three, glorious Tens, sitting in a spread together.

  You may be caught up in a serious state of intellectual or professional struggle, striving to complete a college degree, earn a serious promotion for yourself, or get a new business venture off the ground. When you see a spread containing three Tens, you can rest assured that you are well on your way to achieving prosperity and the degree of happiness and contentment you have been earnestly seeking.

  Consider the fundamental meanings of the Tens: Love, Money, Travel, Business or official matters. Yes, you can read the Tens individually and collectively to interpret their meanings, which will undoubtedly provide you with specific insight. But bear in mind that just viewing three of them in a spread is a strong intuitive sign that your life faces dramatic, uplifting change which you will celebrate and reap considerable joy from in days to come.

- **The Aces:** Whenever you find three Aces in a spread, you are perceiving an extraordinary signpost in your reading in terms of the future. While the Tens in a spread indicate a dynamic thrust

toward the future in a powerful, positive way, three Aces hold
the intuitive message of a "surprisingly delightful turn of events"
perceived to bring new meaning to your life in days to come.

I expect the first thought that comes to your mind in reference
to the Aces is, "How can the Ace of Spades with the apex up ever
be considered to be a delightful surprise?"

Endings, as they are perceived in readings, are not all negative!
In fact, many "endings" (per se) herald the opening of beautiful,
bright new doors to the future. Consider, for instance, the ending
of single life as one enters commitment to marriage. The ending of
a life spent co-habituating with room mates or family members in
favor of a home of your own. The ending of a painful phase in marriage when communication has been seriously lacking, bringing a
fresh start and a renewed sense of commitment between partners.

Whenever you find three Aces in your readings, prepare yourself
for that surprisingly delightful turn of events. View these cards and
think, "Am I in for a wonderfully unexpected surprise!" Three Aces
in a spread are letting you know that your life path, while perhaps
riddled with obstacles and hardships to conquer in the present
moment, holds tremendous promise for favorable change in the
near future.

This prophesy will enable you to see your way through the difficulties of the moment, aware that life holds critical, life-altering
blessings for us, particularly when we least expect them.

- **The Fives:** Consider, for a moment, the meanings of the Fives in
the deck. Three of the Fives are exceedingly good cards – Agreements, News, Gifts. That fourth Five – the Five of Spades (Anger)
– may seem to be quite a destructive force in comparison to the
others.

Intuitively speaking, anger can actually be a very positive, cleansing element in our lives and our relationships with others. Anger
clears the air. It gives us courage to express how we honestly feel.
It generates in us the energy to propel ourselves toward the future
in ways we might never feel we have the power to achieve until we

became truly angry enough to change our own present circumstances.

While we may feel momentarily upset or agitated by those we hardly know who do or say something to irritate us, we only get really angry with those who play significant roles in our lives.

Therefore, the Five of Spades has the ability to guide us in "separating the wheat from the chaff" in our relationships, and it helps us grow emotionally in the process as we strive to resolve our feelings of anger with one another.

You will find in your readings that frequently change won't be initiated until a situation grows so frustrated and fraught with anger that making new choices to bring about change becomes the only alternative. In such instances, you will find the Five of Spades in a spread containing two of the other Fives in the deck, carrying the intuitive message that from anger, new agreements, better communication and/or constructive rewards in terms of the future hold potential to be achieved.

- **Face Cards:** When a spread contains three face cards, rest assured that your social life is on a strong, positive upswing. Three face cards appearing together indicates that a surge of new friends, colleagues, and increased contact with others is swiftly approaching for you.

  Those who have endured a lengthy period of loneliness or a lack of professional recognition for quite some time should perceive such a spread to contain extremely hopeful prophesy in that new opportunities to become productively involved with others are on the way to bring new shape and meaning to their lives.

  Study these three face cards carefully. Take note of which turned in your direction and those cards which are turned away. If all three face cards are turned toward you, consider the message to be that you will share meaningful, close-knit relationships with these individuals who have yet to enter your life. On the other hand, the face cards which are turned away from you, hold the intuitive message that these relationships will be far more casual but nonetheless meaningful stepping stones to a more rewarding, future of being connected with people, in the long run.

When the face card which represents yourself falls in a three-face-card spread, consider this to indicate that you will become very closely involved with the other two depicted by these cards.

A spread containing three face cards provides you with invaluable insight about who will impact your life in the future. More information regarding face cards will be covered in future lessons. For now, focus on the positive, intuitive message that three face cards in a spread offers you in terms of accelerated personal contact with others in the future. This type of spread is Critical in the sense that new individuals entering our lives brings new situations, circumstances and, certainly, greater emotional dimension to our lives in general.

Your training to this point has brought you to an intuitive level where, with some effort, you should be able to view the cards in your reading layout and perceive a certain intuitive "guide word" for yourself from them. This intuitive guide word is not a word or phrase you will plainly see in your reading. It is a word or phrase which comes to you perceptually as you view the cards overall and as you view the spreads individually. The word which surfaces in your mind as you view your cards is your intuitive guide word.

That word or phrase may come to you as "Patience" or "Be cautious", "Loving Spirit" or "Strength." It may be a word you've never actually used in conversation before. If so, look it up in the dictionary. That word or phrase has come to you intuitively and you need to learn its meaning.

Perceiving Intuitive Trends in Readings

Now that you have learned to read individual cards very intently as they are presented to you in spreads, I'm going to take you a crucial step further by teaching you not to read these spreads as intently from now on.

You may be thinking, "What on earth...? I've learned to focus on spreads in order to intuit their messages and now I'm not supposed to?"

Not exactly, so don't despair! Instead of merely following the 1+1+1=__ formula that you have been practicing, intuitively perceiving separate spreads (which have been essentially disconnected from one another), you will now start looking for significant intuitive trends in your spreads as well as the layout itself, overall.

These trends usually aren't specifically spelled out in terms of the 1+1+1=____. They are more your own general perceptions achieved from viewing the cards in the spreads and the layout itself. In other words, rather than simply reading the individual "sentences" contained in your layouts, you're going to now learn to also perceive the meaning of the whole "paragraph" from which you will be able to summarize the messages overall.

I'll warn you, this is not an especially easy step to take. It took me close to two years when I first began to study Personal Prophesy to accurately perceive and invest enough faith in these trends for me to fully trust them, so do be patient with yourself as you take this big step forward in your training.

When you lay the cards down for a reading, chances are that particular spreads are beginning to jump right out at you. You may already possess a deep perception about what you will find in your readings as a direct result of previous readings you've conducted. As the cards fall, you seem to know which cards will most likely surface in certain spreads, and those cards quite frequently, do.

Without perhaps realizing it, you are becoming aware of intuitive trends in your readings – cards which fall as if they are continuing threads in the process of being woven into, say, a big, intuitive piece of fabric as you conduct repeated readings for yourself (or others).

These trends are highly significant in that they are advising you about the future development of your life path. They are telling you that, "These events/situations are on the periphery of your life and while still in the process of taking shape, they hold the potential to become reality for you."

Of course, those potential events/situations may never actually be realized. Advance knowledge of them can cause you to make new choices for yourself – particularly if they are negative future experiences being perceived – altering your future path in the process. Or someone closely connected to these events/situations could choose to make similar choices for him/herself which will directly impact what ultimately becomes reality in terms of these events/situations in the end. More times than not, however, these events/situations will prevail in your readings over and over, advising you that, "This is experience which will inevitably become a part of your life; prepare yourself for it now."

Why this is so, is relatively simple to understand after the weeks, if not months, you have spent working with your cards and gaining expertise with them in your readings: The events/situations you perceive in readings rarely develop out of nowhere, as I'm sure you are discovering as you conduct repeated readings.

It's important to remember that while the placement of the cards is very important in reading spreads, it isn't in terms of the reading layout itself. As you conduct your readings, try not to become fixated on having to interpret what you see in the various layout designations as being solely related to the respective designation they have fallen under. It is much more important to focus on the actual placement of the cards in the spreads themselves.

For instance, when cards fall together in a spread such as this: **Jack of Spades/Seven of Spades/Ten of Hearts** – it means something entirely different, intuitively, than if the cards fell: **Seven of Spades/ Ten of Hearts/Jack of Spades.**

The more attention you pay to the placement of cards in the spreads, the more clarity your readings will contain overall.

The only spreads which directly relate to the question are the wish designation and whichever spread the Nine of Hearts happens to appear in. However, other spreads, particularly when your current situation is an especially weighty one, may relate, if your life is in the process of undergoing massive, dramatic change. Such as following the death of a loved one, an unexpected breakup with your partner, sudden loss of all income, even a horribly upsetting argument with a friend could cause all of the spreads to relate in some way to that question.

Please bear in mind that you are only just beginning to develop a deep, personal link with the cards at this level in your training. As you conduct more and more readings for yourself, you will begin to see trends developing in them. You may be amazed to find the same cards appearing in your readings, in the very same order, again and again and again. Do these readings enough and I guarantee that you will begin to anticipate certain cards falling in a certain order. You will intuitively know in advance what those cards will be. Some of what you start perceiving in these repeated readings might really astound you by how accurately they interpret the development of important situations in terms of your life.

The Impact of Past Experience on Trends in Readings

More times than not, new events and situations are actually the direct result of your own previous experience, or the experience of others as they live their lives. It's as if what develops is merely another link in a big, long chain of experiences that have naturally developed into new experience along the way.

The more you understand about the subtle nuances attached to trends in the reading process and how to decipher them in your layouts, the better equipped you will be to exercise solid decision-making about your own future in the end.

For instance, when you perceive an individual in your readings who harbors bitterness or resentment toward you, you may not initially understand where such feelings originate. But remember, by conducting intuitive readings of this type, you possess the ability to literally peer into the lives of others and see what it is that makes them tick, emotionally as well as psychologically.

That bitterness or resentment didn't suddenly develop straight out of the blue. It had a point of origin somewhere in time. With your cards, you have the ability to fundamentally 'zero in' on where, when and how such feelings came to take root within the heart of this individual. And perhaps most importantly, ascertain the reason you are perceived to be the target for such feelings in the first place.

Perhaps this individual is a close friend or a co-worker you are particularly fond of. In the past, you've shared an extremely pleasant relationship. Now you find yourself perceiving hard feelings on his or her part, feelings you don't readily understand as you conduct your reading.

You should first take a good, long, close look at your layout. Again, bear in mind that this is the part that takes a tremendous amount of practice. What intuitive messages suddenly spring into your mind about this situation? These messages, with practice and concentration, will come to you quite readily in the form of little intuitive lightning bolts of insight:

"She is secretly jealous of me because I have a good marriage and she can't even get a decent man to date her." Or, "He doesn't think I'm worthy of my promotion because he has a college degree and I don't, even though he always tells me how gifted I am." Or, "If I gave more of myself in general emotionally, I wouldn't be so misunderstood so much of the time by those closest to me."

Where do such intuitive lightning bolts come from? They come from your own intuitive perception, of course, as you practice and learn to allow the cards to be the keys which open these startling doors of insight for you.

As a result, you will begin to realize the Past isn't anywhere near as 'dead and gone' as most would like to believe it is. The Past plays an extremely important role in readings, particularly in the sense that who we are today, in the way that we think and feel, and has essentially been shaped by what we've experienced in the Past.

The trend you seein your readings regarding this friend or colleague would be either:

1. Greater understanding about this relationship on your part in the future, bringing you closer in the end as a result, or
2. Your own gradual change-of-heart in the future which would more than likely lead you toward allowing this relationship to come to a close completely.

In other words, as you conduct your readings not only are you looking for the Nine of Hearts in your spreads to provide you with clear, intuitive answers. You are also looking for the more deeply-rooted story behind the story contained in the layout in general.

The more you practice and polish your card-reading skills, the more you will be able to draw these intuitive stories from your cards which will bring greater depth, sharper clarity and more dimensions to your readings as you conduct them.

Homework

Pull together everything you have learned thus far and conduct a full reading for yourself, making it as multi-dimensional as you can. As you view your layout (or layouts, depending on how many you require for this assignment):

1. Make your wish for knowledge, "*Will my life be better than it is at present one year from today?*" Detail in your reading the outcome of this wish.
2. State what you perceive to be your intuitive guide word for this reading.
3. Highlight any Critical cards you may find in your reading.

Chapter Fifteen
A New Layout to Learn

Every aspect of Personal Prophesy you have learned so far has been designed to lead you precisely to this moment. It's a tremendously significant moment. What you are about to learn in this lesson about Personal Prophesy will mean all the difference in the world between a mediocre card reading and one which is truly outstanding in terms of its intuitive depth and accuracy.

Over the course of these lessons we've touched on a wide variety of principles involved in this method. Potential for reality, choice and change as tools for better living. Understanding imagery, degrees of pain and love, processing intuitive information and reading time frames.

We are now about to focus on what I consider to be the most important principle there is in conducting readings by this method: The Power of this Moment.

I'll bet the Present, this "moment" you find yourself currently standing in, isn't one you think is terribly important to your life. Most people, I've discovered, after years and years of reading cards for the public, are so busy living their lives at least two weeks, a month, sometimes even six or more months down the road that they don't have time, let alone the energy, to even ponder how powerful the present is.

Stop and think for a minute. Where are you currently living your life in terms of the past, present and future? If you are truly honest with yourself, you are either:

1. Living your life in the Past – clinging to events and circumstances which have inevitably led you to this particular "moment" where you do not want to focus your attentions.
2. Living your life in the Future –that place in time you yearn will bring the happiness and personal fulfillment you seek, which you do not feel the Present has to offer you.

Very few people in this world actually live their lives in the present, and there is a very good reason why that is. The present – this "*moment*" – is a place in time which generally isn't very gratifying. The present often encompasses pain and hardship, sorrow and regret, or plain drudgery.

It may seem to hold nothing but feelings of emptiness. Inertia. The memory of dreams long since abandoned, better left forgotten, or so you believe. In essence, it is a moment in time seriously considered to be lacking in joy and without joy, the present often seems hardly worth the living.

Most tend to only endure the present in order to either resurrect that experience of joy from the past or to achieve a state of new joy in the future. Those who live their lives in the past or the future view the present as nothing more than a bus stop where they read the paper, twiddle their thumbs or pace frantically, waiting for that all-important, crucial connection to take them somewhere other than "here" and "now".

I have news for you. "Here" – this moment – is an incredibly magical place in time. Who you are, right now, emotionally, intellectually, spiritually, has essentially been shaped by your own past experience and how you've personally processed it over time.

Who you will become in the future takes shape from this moment in the present, where you have the power to learn from the past and move forward productively as a result of that learning. You literally can become someone entirely different in the way you think, feel and believe – if you choose to seize the power of this moment.

This is your moment to spend discovering new facets about yourself, to reflect and understand the nature of your own life better. You can take this moment and reap tremendous wisdom from it. You can seize the power it offers you to direct your future path in the manner you desire it most to go. You can transform yourself into an entirely new person, simply by living fully in the moment and accepting its full reality.

If, on the other hand, you choose not to seize that power, you simply continue to repeat the past in terms of your relationships, your career, your dreams, your own thought processes, suffering considerably (and needlessly) in the process. You can continue to indulge yourself with shallow pleasures, to be a slave to your own fears. You can allow the choices of others to dominate your life and victimize your own happiness, or you can turn those 52 playing cards into serious tools for achieving love, success, happiness – the true qualities of an enriched, rewarding life by intuitively putting this moment to work for you.

Putting The Moment to Work in Your Readings

Whenever you sit down to conduct a reading for yourself, you are viewing your life as it currently stands, as well as the path it is projected to take into the future, at "this moment."

Very little perceived in your readings has been written in stone. As I'm sure you've discovered at some point while taking this course, the future has a tendency to fluctuate as you make choices, and those connected to your life also make choices, from day to day.

Doing Personal Prophesy readings for yourself gives you the opportunity to not only monitor these fluctuations from day to day but to also achieve mastery with them as a result of your own intuitive perception.

What you perceive in your readings are indicators of what is to come. You have the power in many instances to alter that which is perceived to come by possessing this pre-knowledge and acting on it accordingly. As examples:

1. When you perceive upcoming conflicts with your partner, you can take positive steps in the Present to circumvent these conflicts perceived to occur in the Future by establishing better communication, expressing forgiveness or striving toward greater understanding between the two of you to alter the prophesy of that approaching breakup.

2. When you perceive your security in the workplace faces a period of serious jeopardy in the Future, you have the opportunity in the Present to either put forth a higher level of performance on the job or to begin seeking a new position elsewhere, altering your own future path leaning toward dismissal as perceived in the cards as a result.

3. When a future falling-out with a friend is perceived to bring an abrupt halt to your relationship, you are able to put this pre-knowledge to good use by not allowing emotions to get out of hand when a situation arises which seriously threatens the future of the friendship you have shared.

4. When you feel you can't survive a single minute more of the pain, loneliness, lack of opportunity the Present holds for you, the intuitive messages contained in your cards will let you know that you can survive, that if you embrace Hope and look to the future as an open door rather than focusing on those doors which may have closed in the Past for you, the power you seize from the moment you stand in is one of strength and wisdom.

In essence, this moment in the present puts the future at your command, if you heed the intuitive messages in your cards regarding the path you are currently following toward the future. You will discover you are very much in control, if you choose to be, as you conduct your readings and put to use your own pre-knowledge of those events perceived to impact your life quite dramatically.

For now, strive to empower yourself, whenever you conduct your readings, by perceiving the future course of your life path as extremely subject to change as a result of the choices you and those closest to you make daily.

Focus on what you perceive to be solutions to problems/conflicts/situations the cards point out as holding potential for becoming reality in your life. Stretching your intuitive perception to encompass these solutions is an excellent lesson in learning to live in the moment.

Once you become comfortable with this process, you will be well on your way as a knowledgeable, skilled Personal Prophesy card reader.

A New Layout

I am presenting this new layout as a departure from the intensity of the course thus far. You might find this new layout vastly entertaining as it offers you a "quickie" method for conducting intuitive readings.

My grandmother, who taught me this layout, referred to it as The Bed. She would chuckle and describe it as, "Making your own bed and laying in it!" Had she lived long enough, I know she would have been truly delighted to see this layout offered here to people learning Personal Prophesy the world over.

To conduct a reading with this layout, you will need to refer to the instructions below:

1. Select from the deck that face card which represents you or (the recipient) of this reading. Place that card on the table in front of you.

2. Now, shuffle the deck. Fan the cards out on the table in front of you. Select 16 cards from anywhere in the deck and keep them face down, one on top of the other. There is no need to concentrate on a particular "wish". Bed readings are an on-the-spot overview of a person's life. Wishing is not a part of this particular intuitive process.

Note: The first card you choose will be on the bottom, the last card on the top.

3. Place the cards in the layout in the following manner: The top card of the 16 you've selected, position on top of the face card which represents you. Yes, right on top of it, face up. In the dia-

gram, this first card is the Ace of Spades and should be on top of the face card, covering the face card. This card will be interpreted as "What Faces You" when the actual reading is begun.

4. Place the next top card sideways on top of your face card and the Ace of Spades, as represented by the Four of Spades in the diagram. This card will be interpreted as "What Crosses You" for the actual reading.

5. The next card in your hand takes the Seven of Spades position in the diagram. This card will be interpreted as "What Heads You" in the reading.

6. The next card in your hand takes the position of the Queen of Diamonds in the diagram. This card will be interpreted as "What Foots You" in the reading.

7. The next card in your hand takes the position of the King of Spades in the diagram. This card will be interpreted as "What Sides You" in the reading.

8. The next card takes the position of the Nine of Diamonds in the diagram interpreted as "What Guides You" in the reading.

9. Place the next card in your hand in the position of the Ace of Diamonds in the diagram. There are no further special designations given to the remaining cards you hold and will position in the layout.

10. The next card takes the position of the Nine of Clubs in the diagram.

11. The next card takes the position of the Queen of Hearts in the diagram.

12. The next card takes the position of the Eight of Clubs in the diagram.

You now have the cards positioned in a square, with six cards still left to put into the layout. The remaining cards will simply make the square larger with the next step.

13. Place the next card in your hand in the position of the King of Diamonds, the next = Jack of Diamonds, the next = Six of Clubs, the next = King of Hearts, the next = Ten of Diamonds,

and the last card = Five of Clubs.
14. You have now successfully laid out "The Bed."

It is always arranged by these steps. "Bed" readings can be conducted a limitless number of times. You might find it quite amazing to see many of the same cards come up in it, over and over again. Also, any time the Nine of Hearts appears in a layout of "The Bed" consider it to indicate extreme good fortune; specifically, that a cherished wish is destined to come true. (Which I've never seen not happen yet!)

To conduct a reading of "The Bed":

1. Begin with your face card and the card which has been placed on top of it. This top card represents matters in your immediate future – "What Faces You". Read it in the context of what lies ahead in terms of situations, circumstances and individuals.
2. Continue to the card turned sideways. This card represents "What Crosses You" – those individuals, situations, circumstances which stand in your way as impediments to your success and happiness.
3. Proceed to read the card in the position of the Seven of Spades – "What Heads You". This designation involves reading all of the cards in that row from left to right as if it were a five-card spread. These cards encompass all sorts of matters in your life which have yet to be firmly settled. Here you will find a variety of situations, relationships and other circumstances depicted in your cards, offering intuitive insight about aspects to your life which are considered to be "up in the air."
4. Next proceed to the card in the Queen of Diamonds position – "What Foots You." This designation also involves reading all of the cards in that row from left to right, as if it were a five-card spread. These cards encompass recent past events and circumstances which have led you to this moment in time, offering insight into relationships and situations which have developed to the point they have in the Present. You will also see

depicted here those who hold potential to return from the Past, re-entering your life in a most significant way.

5. From here proceed to the card in the King of Spades position. Read this card and the one positioned to its immediate left, as if a two-card spread. This designation, "What Sides You" are those individuals and circumstances which are impacting the decisions you are making in the Present as a result of their emotional, psychological or spiritual influence in your life.

6. From here, proceed to the card in the Ten of Diamonds position. This designation, "What Guides You", is read with the card immediately on its right, comprising a two-card spread. Here you will find intuitive messages regarding those individuals and situations which are perceived in the Present to be instrumental to the future direction of your life's path.

7. Now, read the entire middle row as a spread in a natural progress from the Past (What Sides You) to the Present (your own face card with the two cards on top of it) to the Future (What Guides You.

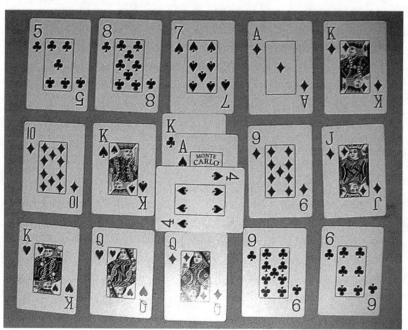

8. Overall, view the layout, noting how many Tens you see, how many Fours you see, whether the Nine of Hearts is present, any other significant trends in the reading. This is a concise, "quickie" reading layout. You may enjoy it for it also you to cut through the excesses of the longer layout and it frequently tends to get right to the heart of a troubling problem.

Homework

1. Conduct a reading for yourself using the original layout, illustrating from it two clear examples of how thinking in terms of the "The Power of the Moment" can help you solve current dilemmas/situations in your own life as you perceive them taking shape for the future. These examples can relate to situations of long or short-term duration.
2. Practice a few "Bed" readings for yourself and others!

Chapter Sixteen
Intuitively Perceiving
the Future for Others

Up to this point, very little information contained in this course has pertained to reading cards for others. Yes, we did a reading for "Gloria" very early on, but it was intended to give you a glimpse of the reading process and the many facets involved. I specifically designed this course to be as such so that one learning from it would concentrate as much as possible on reading the cards to gain the most in terms of personal rewards from this training.

You have progressed to a level of awareness where it is now time to expand your skills and begin learning to read cards belonging to other people. Doing so will bring a whole new dimension to your own readings overall. The first step in learning to accurately read cards belonging to others is conducting readings "by proxy."

Reading cards "by proxy" essentially means you are reading cards belonging to someone else without having them sitting right beside you, physically present to participate in these readings. You can accomplish such a feat with or without their knowledge – these readings are no less valid than your own readings or those you conduct when others are present. Regardless of whether these individuals are aware these readings are being conducted in reference to their own lives, "proxy" readings make it possible for you to obtain an accurate, intuitive view into these lives as others are actually living them.

To conduct a "proxy" reading, you shuffle the cards focusing on a mental image of the individual whose cards you wish to read. Don't attempt to cut the cards or place them into the layout until you have achieved that crucial, clear-cut image of this individual in your own mind. This step can take anywhere from 10 seconds to five minutes.

Whenever I personally conduct such readings, I think very carefully about the individual and wait until I feel a certain sense of calm or peace envelope me, letting me know that I have successfully created this mental image before I begin the reading process. Once you feel you are just as fully focused on the individual whose cards you are about to read, prepare to make your wish for knowledge by placing your hands on the deck and saying to yourself: "These cards belong to (Name). I am wishing to know from his/her cards...." then proceed to make your specific wish for knowledge.

As you place the cards in the layout, always bear in mind that these cards belong only to that individual. While you are in a position to read them, you should never assume you have any role to actively play in the reading or that you impact this individual's life in any way.

The more unattached and emotionally objective you can be in your perceptions of readings conducted "by proxy", the more accurate your perceptions will be in the long run. This aspect to correctly perceiving "proxy" readings cannot be stressed enough: No matter how close you may think you are to another individual, when you read their cards "by proxy", you stand on the outside looking in 100 percent of the time.

In other words, the cards which lay before you are their cards exclusively. You must not attempt to project your involvement with this person into the reading. You must not superimpose your own value system into the reading. You must remain totally objective in terms of your intuitive viewpoint or the reading simply will not be valid.

As you conduct "proxy" readings, remember: You are not the one who stands to the left of each spread as you do in readings that are your own. You are reading each spread as if you were that individual you are reading the cards for.

The intuitive insights you receive from "proxy" readings will often truly astound you. These readings offer you the opportunity to literally climb into the mind and heart of another person, to view life from his or her personal perspective, to understand what essentially makes these people tick.

At first, you may feel compelled to conduct "proxy" readings on everybody you know. I did the same thing myself, many years ago. As you become more experienced with your cards and you develop deep respect for your own ability to accurately read them, you may decide to make it your own personal practice to conduct these readings whenever you begin new relationships, question the soundness of an ongoing relationship or wish to inquire about relationships in the past.

"Proxy" readings are remarkably accurate – but do conduct them with care. And be prepared: What you perceive in these readings may tell you more than you ever wanted to know about the private side of those who impact your life, particularly in the emotional sense!

Conducting Professional Readings for Others

Once you feel comfortable conducting readings by "proxy", you are certainly ready to put your intuitive perception to the test by conducting live, one-on-one readings formally for others.

I guarantee that your first, early "clients" will be fascinated by your ability and more than eager to be recipients of your Personal Prophesy insights. You may have already attempted to conduct these readings on your own; if so, you have undoubtedly discovered how delightfully intriguing others find these readings when you offer to intuitively perceive the future for them!

The following tips are designed to guide you as you continue to practice and polish your skills, making it possible for you to conduct readings for others professionally and with ease.

1. Realize that every client you conduct readings for is an individual who views life differently. The worst mistake you can make as a new card reader is to make sweeping judgments, intuitively,

morally or otherwise, where your clients' perceptions about life (theirs in particular) are concerned.

You will find yourself conducting readings for people who come from all walks of life: Rich/poor, educated/uneducated, spiritual/non-spiritual, different cultures/races, those who are heterosexual/ homosexual. In order for your readings to be accurate, you must maintain an open mind while viewing the cards of these people, interpreting the intuitive messages the cards offer you with the utmost compassion and respect.

Any time you sit down to conduct a reading for someone, you are viewing cards which belong to no one *but* that particular individual. The nuances in his/her readings are going to be just as individual. With experience, you will learn to pick up on these nuances and know how to interpret them in your readings correctly.

Until you've achieved that level of mastery with your cards, however, I advise you to stick to the basics and keep your readings focused on the immediate moment – the Present – refraining from attempting to describe personality characteristics, intuitively defining incidents in the Past which have impacted the Present, or making any long-range projections into the Future of any kind.

2. Don't feel pressured to read any layout you don't feel comfortable enough to read. It isn't uncommon to shuffle, cut and arrange the cards for a reading only to find yourself feeling completely disconnected intuitively from the cards which come to lay on the table before you.

    Should this happen as you are attempting a reading for someone else, scan the various spreads to see if you pick up on any intuitive messages, here or there, in the layout which may be useful to remember when you actually conduct that individual's reading. Then simply put the cards back into the deck.

    Your client will patiently wait for you to re-shuffle, cut and arrange the cards. I often repeat this process two, three, even four times until I am 100 per cent certain that I have made the right connection to that individual's life. I simply tell my client that I am establishing that all-important intuitive link.

You may also find that on some days, your intuitive sense is definitely turned "on"; other days, definitely turned "off". Your ability to perceive is bound to fluctuate – you might even find yourself becoming a little eccentric about these fluctuations in the process!

For instance, an outstanding student of mine who has gone on to do a marvelous job of conducting readings for the public in past years is, to this day, convinced she cannot accurately conduct readings when the sky is overcast. Her intuitive ability is somehow impeded by cloud cover, she insists. Another believes her best readings occur during vivid thunderstorms. You may find yourself entertaining such atmospheric tendencies yourself. In my view, it is all a part of the natural order of things – one day we are up, another day down and so on.

3. A client's emotional personality will profoundly affect your ability to comfortably read his or her cards. Because we are all so vastly different from one another, your ability to successfully read cards for others will depend on your own ability to perceive with ease their emotions, which will fluctuate tremendously from person to person.

Here are some good rules of thumb for determining the emotional "depth" of your clients, at this point in your training:

- A layout that contains a significant number of cards that are emotional in nature (regardless of their placement in the layout), signifies an individual who tends to be more emotionally-influenced (or guided) as he or she lives life. Focus your reading so that it is primarily on an emotional level in such a case.
- A layout that contains a significant number of cards that are not emotional in nature (regardless of their placement in the layout), signifies an individual who tends to be more

intellectually-led and may even have difficulty expressing emotions in general. Focus your reading to be on a more logical, intellectualized level in such a case.

- When you find yourself experiencing difficulty intuitively receiving the messages of the various spreads in a layout for a client, consider the possibility that this individual is of extremely high intellect or using personal thought processes that are quite complex. Several layouts and considerable time spent on each spread may be required to successfully read for a client with this type of nature. Don't get discouraged. In time, you will come to understand such complex people and their cards quite well.

- In extremely rare instances, you will find yourself viewing layouts for clients which either make no intuitive sense at all to you or cause you to feel so intensely apprehensive about conducting the reading, you feel you cannot proceed. In such instances, consider the individual to be "unreadable" and decline the request for a reading. Again, this is a very rare occurrence with clients. In all my years, I have only declined reading requests for two clients I considered to be truly "unreadable."

4. Always begin your readings with the same informational format. Remind your clients at the outset of their readings that:
   - You are perceiving their lives at this moment which is subject to change as they make choices which affect their lives from day to day.
   - Explain that while a considerable amount of your perceptions will be startlingly accurate about the future, you are only capable of perceiving the path each client appears to be taking toward the future. None of your statements, therefore, are cast in stone as "This will happen." Ensure that your clients leave a reading with the feeling that no matter what intuitive information you've offered them, they still are essentially in control of their own destinies.

5. Be gentle in the delivery of your perceptions to others. Remember, they are hanging on your every word so do be kind and considerate with your perceptions.

   As your ability to read cards for others increases in accuracy, you will undoubtedly become amazed at some of the shocking revelations the cards will contain for your clients.

   A newlywed friend may come to you for a reading walking on Cloud Nine, yet you perceive clearly from her cards that her new marriage is not going to last. A male co-worker may ask you for a reading and from his cards, you perceive he will soon be fired. A seemingly-content and happy relative may sit down for a reading, but all you perceive is doom and gloom for the future.

   As you become more experienced, you will know how to handle such calamities in your readings. At this point in your training, I advise that you don't blurt out such perceptions to your clients, which will only cause them to walk away from their readings filled with despair. Instead, guide them to be prepared for the inevitable "ups and downs" life will bring their way. For instance:

- When reading for that newlywed friend, remind her that all marriages require effort, that as she and her new husband settle into married life, communication and understanding will be the key to resolving any differences in the future. She will come to you for another reading when her marriage has entered troubled waters, and you will be in a better position at that time to advise her about the possibility of divorce.

- When reading for that co-worker facing losing his job, tell him he faces change and encourage him to turn his career toward the future, to become more open to new opportunity. Remind him that he has gifts and talents he has not been able to put to use in this job and embracing new opportunity will help him make the most of his abilities in the future. He will want another reading when his career change becomes imminent due to his dismissal.

- When that relative wants a reading from you, don't focus

on the "doom and gloom" in the reading but rather, inspire him or her to feel sincerely hopeful about the future, to have enough faith that a better future is on the horizon once current difficulties have been overcome.

You'd be amazed what the right "seeds" can do when they are planted in the minds of those who comes to you for readings and you find yourself faced with painful, disastrous cards.

Attaining The Impossible

We all know people who believe that anything wished for strongly enough could be attained. I wouldn't necessarily call these people unrealistic about life. They're basically caring people who desperately want something to come true for themselves, and they're willing to work for it or sit down and wait for it.

Can the impossible be attained? I'm inclined from my experience with the cards to say no. The prophesy of the cards is quite precise when it comes to matters that involve restrictions or limitations that we simply don't have the ability to change. If it has no potential for becoming reality, there is simply no way what is wished for will actually become reality.

You can't make something happen through force, manipulation, or even just wishing to make it so unless it already has the potential for becoming reality. When it doesn't, the cards will give you this message over and over: "This desire is not an option. You must make another choice. This plan, this dream, this expectation will never be realized. It simply cannot be."

This is where so many tend to have the most difficulty, accepting what has been perceived as impossible. They hear the prophesy of the cards, but they refuse to listen and act on it. They continue to pursue relationships and elusive lovers who have no potential for becoming reality. What ultimately happens? They find themselves wallowing in misery needlessly. By clinging to something that simply doesn't have the potential to become reality, they turn their backs on the genuine, loving relationships the cards offer as real opportunities for lasting future happiness.

Just as you must accept the reality of your situation, you must also accept the reality of your desires. Choose to find the right kind of happiness for yourself, rather than trying to make the impossible happen. With the cards as your guide, you can learn to avoid relationships that will only cost you in terms of suffering and sorrow. And you can guide your clients just as expertly.

If there is another man or woman standing between your client and the person he or she loves; if they are trying to captivate and marry a certain person who has not even met them yet; if a client wants an old lover to return to his or her life – these are not necessarily "impossibilities." It would depend greatly on the circumstances surrounding these individuals at that precise moment in time and the personal inclinations of the other parties involved.

One thing is certain, the cards are extremely reliable when it comes to revealing exactly what the future holds in store should you choose to pursue a relationship along these lines, and they will let you know just what your chances really are for succeeding.

Listen to these messages when you get them from the cards. They are important ones as you travel your own personal path to happiness. Impossible dreams are just that – impossible. Give them a nice, quick mercy killing and simply let these dreams die. You'll be far better off, in the long run, without them.

A Few Important Nuances about the Cards

Here are but a few of the important nuances you will learn as you continue to gain expertise perceiving the future in your readings:

1. During the shuffling process or placing the cards into the layout, should a card suddenly fall on the floor, pick it up and read it. This card bears special meaning for you at that particular moment in your life. My grandmother used to say whenever a card fell from the deck as she was preparing to conduct a reading, "If it falls on the floor, it comes to the door." In other words, this

card is offering you a significant intuitive message in terms of your life and the reading you are about to conduct.

2. When you are conducting a reading for someone and you find yourself experiencing great difficulty picking up on their emotions as well as perceiving the path they are following to the future, intuitively speaking, you are dealing with an extremely complex personality. This individual is more intellectual by nature than the average person, not prone to express emotion freely and will not be an easy subject for a reading. Assume a more analytical approach to the reading and you will put yourself in a far better position to tap in on the life of this particular client.

3. When you perceive an individual bearing the Four of Hearts in your readings, don't merely perceive the jealousy on his or her part – look intuitively beyond it. This person is experiencing jealousy due to their own deep-seated feelings of inferiority, insecurity, lack of personal identity. By reading the story behind the story, you enable yourself to achieve a deeper understanding of their motivations for feeling as they do.

4. The Ace of Diamonds doesn't always just indicate "marriage" in your readings. When this card falls into a spread where there are no face cards present, it indicates your committed partner or the one your heart perceives will become your future mate.

Homework

Here's your chance to really shine!

1. Conduct a few by "proxy" readings for people you know extremely well, just for your own personal practice. When you feel comfortable enough with this process, conduct a reading by "proxy" for a celebrity or a world figure, check your insights by reading about them in magazines or current-event web sites.

2. Conduct a live, one-on-one reading with someone you would consider to be a "client" (friend, relative, co-worker).

Chapter Seventeen
Living Life
More Intuitively

When we are mired in indecision about the future and reluctant to make choices for ourselves, there's an important reason involved: Timing. Most fail to take this vital element – timing – into account as they live their lives, failing to realize that they encounter the obstacles they do so that their life paths will ultimately turn in the right direction as a result.

After all these years of studying Personal Prophesy, I'm convinced that readings, relationships, new jobs, the conceiving of children, buying homes – nothing essentially happens until it is within the realm of its own timing. Yes, you can persevere and strain yourself to try to make these events occur sooner than now. But would it be the road to the future you were meant to take, despite the perseverance and the strain? I personally don't believe so.

As I often explain in readings to others who are waiting for certain events to take place, I am a firm believer that circumstances present us with hardships for a very important reason: Timing. When the moment itself is not correct for a specific event to occur, obstacles will suddenly present themselves to hold us back, unexpectedly delaying and detaining us from moving forward – even in terms of something as seemingly simple as finding a new job or a place to live.

We can force these events and strain like crazy to make them happen, but without timing on our side, those forced events are very much like cakes that have been taken out of the oven too soon. While it may look like a cake and smell like a cake, the instant you cut into it you can tell that cake wasn't anywhere near ready to leave the oven.

In view of this, a large percentage of readings will fall under the Personal Prophesy principle of timeliness – something most people fail to take into account as they live their lives. In other words, the aspects we perceive about our lives perceived as "coming in the future" are actually being delivered to us in what is considered to be the most appropriate time for their creation and completion. Because there are no obstacles to hold these events from opening new doors to the future for us when the time is correct, we will be able to reap far greater happiness and fulfillment from them.

When I sit down to read the cards for someone, the intuitive messages I receive from them are coming to me in what I believe is their most appropriate time. What was read in the cards two weeks ago is really quite irrelevant. It's what can be perceived from them now that is the most important.

That sense of "now" is the essence of timeliness. Even though the moment is fluid and ever-changing, it still is realistically the only moment you really have to work with as you move toward the future from "now" to "now" to "now" and so on.

I know this is a very complicated aspect to reading the cards that most fail to comprehend because it is so difficult to grasp. With time and experience, you will come to understand why some events happen quickly and easily and others seem riddled with obstacles and delays. Those obstacles are intended to bring these events into their own "time" which isn't necessarily your "time" or my "time" but the timing most appropriate for them to become reality within the framework of your life.

Capacity for Success

Capacity for success. These three words carry a tremendous amount of weight in terms of our professional lives. Capacity for success is defined as our own maximum potential to experience and appreciate success, particularly in terms of individual ambitions and dreams.

Those who haven't realized their true capacity for success are intuitively perceived in Personal Prophesy readings as merely making a living. Those who have realized their capacity for success, however, are wholeheartedly committed to reaping tremendous personal rewards for themselves. They receive these benefits from a vocation or "calling", making a significant contribution to the world in the process.

Capacity for success isn't defined by money, power or position. It isn't about earning college degrees, gaining promotions or in any way being officially acknowledged for accomplishments on your part. It is completely centered on *you* and your ability to define "success" in terms of your own life, without comparing it or shaping it in relation to anyone else's.

Imagine that as we each go about the business of living our individual lives, we are carrying a bucket around with us. This bucket symbolizes our own individual capacity to experience success. It enables us to actually feel successful within the framework of our lives.

It doesn't matter how large or small that bucket is that we're carrying. Full is full, empty is empty. How "full" or how "empty" isn't relative to the size of my bucket next to yours. Your bucket is only connected to your life. Nobody else's bucket matters. In your bucket is a great deal of water , or, perhaps, very little water. This depends on how much or how little of your own *capacity for success* you've realized for yourself.

Consider: A man sells who shoes for a living but wishes he was building and selling beautiful houses would have very little water in his bucket. He has simply not realized his true capacity for success. Now, he may be considered by others to be a "successful" salesman. He may even outsell every other shoe salesman in town consistently every month. But if he doesn't experience any genuine sense of *success* for himself while selling those shoes, intuitively speaking, he would be perceived as not being very successful at all. He is essentially making a living, probably an unhappy one at that.

Without experiencing personal fulfillment from his job selling shoes, being the best shoe salesman in town is, at least for this man, a rather empty accomplishment indeed.

You might think, "Why doesn't he just go ahead and build and sell the homes he wants to, so he will feel successful?"

While life, on the intuitive level, is an immense sea of opportunity and possibility, it also tends to be characterized by nothing but real or imagined obstacles and restrictions to the average person. Such obstacles and restrictions hold us back from making our dreams come true and realizing our true capacities for success. The largest of which tends to be fear – particularly the fear that we might be incredibly *UN*-successful, should we venture from our safe, little world of mediocrity. Still, as I have found to so often be the case as a result of intuitive perception, exactly the opposite occurs once we find t he courage to take that step.

Consider, for example, the experience of a female client of mine who came to me for intuitive guidance. She was an elementary school teacher and had been for several years. However, in her reading, I perceived that teaching was only a "job" to her: Simply the way she made her living. Even though she had gone to college and earnestly sought a career in teaching, she was reaping absolutely no personal sense of fulfillment from her work as a teacher. Her bucket, where capacity for success is concerned, contained very little water.

It turned out that she always wanted to be a professional singer and, in fact, had a truly gorgeous voice. She often went on stage in various clubs to sing with bands that were performing but never made a personal commitment to actively pursue a career in singing for what the cards indicated was a rather superficial reason.

This particular woman thought she was too overweight to even risk the possibility of being unsuccessful as a professional singer. She basically chose to hide her true ambitions behind the veil of elementary school teaching.

I perceived from the cards, however, that her capacity for success, what would literally fill her bucket right to the top, was to actively pursue this singing career. Not only was this move seen in her reading as a very successful and extremely fulfilling career change, she would also become a rather well known, local talent as a result.

As a result of her reading, I strongly encouraged this woman to make that change.

It took some time – about a year – before she was willing to trust the prophesy of the cards. She eventually took steps to realize her true capacity for success, despite what she considered her own personal obstacle in terms of success – her weight.

I am very pleased to say that today she is the lead singer of her own musical group and her bucket – her capacity for success – is running over.

An extraordinary situation?

Not at all. I couldn't begin to tell you how many people I've read for over the years who, ultimately, achieved their own capacities for success because of their own willingness to believe in the intuitive prophesy of the cards. They had enough faith to strive to make those personal dreams become reality.

Think about your own life for a moment. Where are you in terms of your "capacity for success"? How "full" or how "empty" is your bucket? If you consider your bucket to be "full," you are an individual who has obviously recognized at some point in your life what your true ambitions were and set out in a rather determined fashion to realize those ambitions for yourself. If you consider your bucket to be very far from full and you are basically just making a living, this is not a satisfying, fulfilling way to live.

Maybe you are a homemaker who has always dreamed of being an interior decorator. While homemaking put some water in your bucket, making the commitment and actively pursuing a career as an interior decorator would literally fill it to the top. You would be perceived in the cards as engaged in a career that genuinely fulfills you.

You might be a well-respected lawyer earning a tremendous amount of money. You may even turn clients away because you are considered that "successful." If you crawl home from your office every night feeling drawn, exhausted, and frustrated, your bucket would be far from full. If you were you to give up law, however, and follow your dream of, say, writing Harlequin romances, your bucket would fill up like crazy.

Capacity for success, therefore, is the true essence of your own dreams, desires, and aspirations. It is focused on "who" you really are in terms of making a personally gratifying contribution from within yourself to the world in general.

Intuitively speaking, most people walk through life never even coming close to realizing their own true capacity for success. They satisfy themselves as best they can by settling for opportunities to simply become "gainfully employed" in a monetary sense. They do so, rather than risk striving to achieve their deepest dreams and desires, which literally spring from inside the heart. These people find themselves enduring a tremendously unrewarding existence as a result.

It doesn't have to be that way. We all possess the power to realize our own true capacity for success every day by just being willing to follow our dreams and make them become reality within the framework of our lives.

Take yourself back, right now, to the days of your own youth when you dreamed beautiful dreams of what you wanted to be when you grew up. What caused those dreams to become buried, lost, or perhaps even stolen from you over the years? Maturity? Responsibility? A fear of failure? Or was it that others insisted that you "couldn't"? Only you know the real answer to these questions.

If those dreams are still alive within you – and they always come through quite clearly in an intuitive reading, why not choose to make the necessary shift in your life's path to follow them? What do you honestly have to lose if you do?

Most people are delighted and plainly overjoyed to find that once they do commit themselves to their dreams, when they concentrate on filling that bucket they are carrying right to the top their lives become tremendously enriched and gratifying.

They inevitably come to realize that the contribution they have to make to the world is so meaningful there isn't a paycheck in the world that can compensate for such a genuine feeling of fulfillment.

This is indeed true "capacity for success."

Critical Points of Change

People often approach me and say, "My life has changed so much. I don't understand how I ended up 'here' instead of where I thought I would be today."

The average person doesn't realize that what causes our paths to the future to change so dramatically are frequently the choices we make for ourselves – or the choices others make in reference to their own lives. These choices critically affect our lives in terms of the future.

Critical points of change are often perceived in Personal Prophesy readings long before they take the shape of reality.

Marriages hold critical points of change. Work environments do as well. Our relationship with family members is yet another, not to exclude friendships. Even something as seemingly harmless as choosing to take a vacation can produce a critical point of change. Let's take a closer look at what may catapult us down new paths to the future as a result of critical points of change.

Marriage: People tend to view marriage when they enter into it as a gleaming expanse of highway leading toward a beautiful, romantic, and richly blessed future to be shared together. Unfortunately, marriage isn't that effortless. Marriage is, in actuality, a rough, rut-ridden road that two people travel and hope to conquer together. Once the bloom is off that wedding rose, couples find themselves putting forth great effort to meet day-to-day responsibilities. They cope with financial struggles, relationship conflicts, and the stress of raising children. They are essentially compelled to adjust to and accept human imperfection in their partners or change results. By not being able to accept and adjust in order to keep those marriages strong, they willfully gravitate toward a critical point of change.

Two imperfect people who come together and commit to marriage will never be able to achieve perfection in their relationship, no matter how hard they may try. What they learn in the process of living and grappling with love's deep complexities are difficult lessons in humility and compassion as well as understanding and forgiveness.

Marriage forces us to extend ourselves in terms of loving, emotionally growing and maturing in the process.

Whenever we find we can't extend ourselves in order to be able to give more than what we feel we are receiving, or when we can't handle the stresses or the ups and downs of what we perceived would be a "perfect" union, a critical point of change takes shape. And from it, entirely new futures are naturally formed.

A wife may choose to have an extra-marital affair with a partner she perceives to be more loving, and more attentive to her needs. By doing so she grows away from her husband emotionally, and she points herself toward a new path to the future.

A husband may choose to bury himself in his work rather than cope with his frustration over seemingly insurmountable problems at home. By doing so he steadily loses his focus on his marriage, and by choosing to escape through work, he radically alters the direction his life is taking toward the future. Divorce is a critical point of change.

Illness, Accidents, and Death: As hard as we may try to maintain a happy, healthy, and safe existence, one of these three will inevitably have an impact upon our lives at some point. A loved one may suddenly be diagnosed with cancer. A spouse may wave goodbye from the driveway, only to be killed minutes later in an accident on the interstate. A son goes swimming and becomes a paraplegic from one reckless dive. A daughter contracts AIDS from a boyfriend. You may discover as a result of a routine physical that you have less than a year to live.

These are all critical points of change, bringing important life lessons our way that will profoundly affect our futures. We are forced to face and cope with these life-altering changes in order to achieve a deeper inner strength and a higher level of understanding about life from our ultimate acceptance of these human tragedies.

One of the most basic principles of Personal Prophesy is, "Give the best of yourself in the present moment." In other words, strive to repair conflict-ridden relationships in your life today. Express your love freely to family members and friends. Extend forgiveness to those who need it from you, now. Appreciate your health and the many blessings life has bestowed upon you and your families.

The *tomorrow* that you are counting on to help you resolve pain in your relationships, or to allow you the opportunity to show your love and give from your heart and live life to the fullest may never come. It's what you do with this beautiful, powerful, and wonderful moment you stand in right now – *today* – that counts. Not that elusive tomorrow you may be relying on to make this moment right.

You: That's right, "you" are a critical point of change in terms of your own life. Every single day you make choices that hold the potential to radically affect your path to the future.

You may choose to suddenly change professions or to move to another part of the country. You may conceive a child or choose to abort one you've already conceived. You may decide to quit drinking or using drugs. You may reunite with a family member, or you may come out of the closet and proclaim your homosexuality.

You may choose not to be promiscuous anymore or to go back to school. You may commit yourself to making your marriage work or to leave an exceedingly unhealthy one. You may also courageously accept the challenges life has thrust into your path as you cope with a serious tragedy.

If you find yourself saying, "I don't know how I ended up 'here' instead of where I thought I would be today," reflect on your past, the life you've been living from minute to minute. You'll undoubtedly find that you are exactly where you are supposed to be as a result of your own life experiences and critical points of change that led you directly to this moment.

Intuitive Insights Regarding Emotional Baggage

Let's focus for a moment on a word we all know well. A word we tend to toss between us in discussions with each other, particularly in reference to our relationships with partners, those both past and present, as if it were an overly inflated conversational basketball.

A word that speaks of roadblocks that never fails to appear and impede our own progress toward achieving personal happiness, even when we try our darndest to avoid them. A word recipients frequently receive from me in readings to describe difficulties they are encountering at that particular point in their lives.

That word is *baggage*. Specifically, emotional baggage, the kind we (or our partners) spend years trying to get rid of and yet, inevitably drag like an overstuffed suitcase behind us everywhere we go.

Like ghosts, this baggage relentlessly rises from the past to haunt us, no matter how hard we may try to outrun it. It stays hot on our tails as we speed down the highways of our lives in frantic attempts to evade it. It holds the power to insidiously influence, hamper and outright derail our lives as we strain and struggle to achieve new futures for ourselves.

Face it; every human being on this planet possesses emotional baggage of one kind or another. Whether it's from past relationships, marriages, and our own upbringing as children, we've all got our own fair share of baggage. Baggage we will all carry with us until we consciously confront it and successfully resolve it – or we die.

Those who claim to "travel light" in life are probably carrying the most baggage of all. The problem is, these individuals don't consciously recognize their own baggage as they busy themselves with tedious details while traveling their own life paths, emotionally dabbling here and there with relationships, convincing themselves that they don't need anyone.

However, beneath the transient emotional natures of such individuals, as I've discovered in readings, lies a heart so riddled with pain and fear of rejection that the mere thought of planting roots anywhere emotionally is more than these "light travelers" can realistically bear.

I find a large percentage of women with emotional baggage in readings are running toward something – new relationships or extramarital affairs, new jobs or exotic, distant locations – whatever they feel will immediately rescue them and prevent them from having to deal with their own unresolved issues attached to the past. It never seems to cross their minds that the baggage they are trying to be rescued from will inevitably follow them wherever they go.

Conversely, a large percentage of men, tend to be running away from something – dissatisfying relationships or marriages, unsuccessful careers or financial problems, sexual inadequacy, their own low self esteem. While they may hold back from physically taking steps to abandon and change for themselves such unhappy circumstances, they tend instead to pour their energy into trying to escape their own emotional baggage – if only in for a little while.

By comforting themselves through such avoidance mechanisms as affairs, workaholism, drinking and taking drugs, in some instances, outright denial of the baggage they carry, they ultimately only run right back into their own deep unhappiness in the long run.

The focus between the sexes may be different, but the end result is still the same: We can run but never hide from our own emotional baggage.

It's important to remember that whenever we engage in new relationships these partners come to us with baggage from the relationships they have left behind. My perception is always that while a new partner may grow to care intensely for us, he still carries emotional baggage from that previous relationship which he has yet to resolve for himself, within himself. It's our job to give these new partners the time they need to fully resolve and decisively leave that baggage where it realistically belongs, behind them.

As I've learned over the years as a result of conducting Personal Prophesy readings for hundreds of others, whenever a long-term relationship disintegrates, we must allow ourselves enough time in which to heal and emotionally process the past. By overlapping relationships too quickly, all we really manage to do is push aside that baggage as we enthusiastically try to embrace a new situation. Then we find that baggage will come back to haunt us intensely, only because we are not able to fully commit ourselves to a new future, unencumbered emotionally, as a result of it.

The bottom line is, you can't help a person get rid of their baggage. You can sit down and talk with them until you are blue in the face and they will still have it, carry it, and even cling to it. Why? Because our own baggage and our ability to cope with it plays a critical role in the process toward deep, personal growth. In other words, that loathsome baggage we carry with us is an integral part of our own individual journeys into Becoming who we will be for the future.

As much as I would love to tell you that the best relationships in life are the "easy" ones, unfortunately that is not the case. The more difficult they are, the more worthwhile they ultimately turn out to be in the long run. The more we are able to learn from these relationships as we bring meaningful resolve to our own baggage, the more we are able to become emotionally stronger and healthier for the right partners for us.

Dealing with Family Disputes

Let's discuss effectively coping with family disputes and how the intuitive insight Personal Prophesy offers can help ease conflict within the family. Family relationships are spiritually nurturing at their best and downright impossible to cope with at their worst. What we share with family members should be some of the most celebrated experiences of our lives, but a large number of us can't find enough excuses to escape the very people to whom we are related.

Over the years, I have perceived many more poor family relationships than I have strong ones. I have seen brother pitted against brother, sisters lashing out at sisters, and mothers and fathers who are so emotionally detached from the families they have created that they have no idea why there is conflict and disharmony occurring within them at all.

Intuitively speaking, most parents have a tendency to "sleepwalk" through the raising of their children. They provide the necessities of food, shelter, and clothing. They teach their children what they feel they ought to be taught in terms of society's standards. They take their children to school, give them Christmas presents, enforce house rules, and they send them out into the world once they have reached the age of adulthood. They automatically do all the things they feel they are supposed to do as parents, but are oblivious in their sleepwalking to the most important lesson in life they could ever possibly teach their children: Teach them how to truly love unconditionally.

Think about it. Most of us never had the chance to learn genuinely how to "love" from the people we were born to and inevitably raised by. We grew up in families that attempted to observe major holidays and important occasions with a sense of loving unity, then reverted to arguing and, quite often, shunning each other the remainder of the year.

We grew up in fatherless or motherless homes where the lessons we learned about love were often biased and lopsided. We may have had aunts or grandmothers who raised us without caring for us. There were parents who refused to let us play with children who had the wrong background or skin that was the wrong color. We often learned that forgiveness meant getting a verbal, if not a physical, beating first and having to crawl our way meekly back into the good graces of the family later.

Is it any wonder so many of us experience difficulty with our family relationships today? Without a solid foundation of love, genuine and unconditional love, conflicts between family members are sure to erupt and further erode what should be some of the most important relationships in our lives.

Whenever the cards are intuitively read, the past, when we are focusing on family relationships, must be considered in order for the present and future to be accurately perceived. We must always remember that we are the sum total of our own experiences. Our relatives are the sum total of their own. Because we all process experience differently, we are naturally going to see particular situations from our own individual points of view.

Disputes, therefore, are inevitable, given our own personal perception of the situation, which happens to be at hand. Try, if you can, to look beyond the immediate conflict, to perceptually delve into the emotional make-up of the relative you are at odds with. Chances are that by doing so, you will better understand why he or she has taken such a position, and you will be more apt to find a workable solution between you.

If, for instance, your relations dislike the man or woman you have chosen to marry, take the time to consider why they might feel this way. It probably isn't "him" or "her" causing the conflict between you, but an issue that runs much deeper. If you have serious problems getting along with your mother or father, consider what might be at the root of the difficulty. Is it really "you" or perhaps a personal emotional struggle he or she has yet to resolve. If a sister or brother won't speak to you, refuse to be rejected by sending letters, cards, and calling at every opportunity.

By demonstrating unconditional love toward family members, you have a far better opportunity to help bring them to the point of constructive change, which is what Personal Prophesy is all about.

Disputes between family members require great care in their handling and an abundance of unconditional love on your part so that they can become stronger relationships in the end. You don't have to accept a legacy of conflict and pain in terms of your relationships with family members.

If you choose to be the one who breaks those emotional chains of the past, and persevere through love and forgiveness, you will in time succeed.

Chapter Eighteen
Matters of the Heart

Using Personal Prophesy

Ask yourself if you are making the most of your love life. If you are currently in a good, solid relationship, my hunch is that you will say, "Yes, I most certainly am making the most of my love life."

If you are in a less-than-satisfactory relationship, you're probably thinking, "Well, things could be a lot better, but rather than go back to living without a partner, I'm making the most of what I've got right now, at least until someone better for me comes along."

If you are in a terribly unhappy relationship, or if you are not involved in a romantic relationship at all, you're probably thinking, "No, I'm not making the most of my love life." What it all boils down to at this particular moment in your life is how you perceive your own romantic happiness.

Try to answer these questions:

- Do you see your love life in realistic terms or through the rose-colored glasses of wishful thinking?
- Can you assess what you see as a genuine fulfillment at a time in your life that needs emotional improvement?
- Are you actually gravitating toward lasting happiness or stagnating in a relationship that is not going anywhere?

You may even, plainly speaking, be floundering like crazy just to feel some sort of happiness for yourself at all.

This is where Personal Prophesy comes in. Because this philosophy is so intensely focused on the intuitive perception of emotions, the cards have the capacity to be extremely clear-cut about where you actually are, emotionally, as you follow your own personal life path toward the future.

I'll tell you right now, the cards won't ever lead you down the primrose path of wishful thinking where your love life is concerned. In terms of the cards, wishful thinking is a grand illusion that deceives you into believing what you want to be true is true, and it ultimately puts you at the mercy of the choices being made by those living their lives around you.

The cards prefer to deal with reality rather than fantasy when it comes to love. The cards won't feed your ego, tell you fanciful bedtime stories about your relationships, or give you any sort of false hope about the success of the path you have chosen to take to seek love and happiness. The cards will plainly reveal to you that if you continue to pursue a relationship with a man or woman who does not have the potential to make you truly happy, you will only find yourself brokenhearted and miserable in the end.

The cards will alert you to avoid potential partners who are essentially incapable of fidelity when in committed relationships. They can help you better understand the reasons why a partner has, for instance, suddenly lost heart or is experiencing personal emotional difficulties regarding a relationship.

They can also literally point the way toward those relationships that will make you feel happiest and most complete in the end.

Those who are in good, solid relationships need to remember that these relationships are in fact "living things." Right now, think of your relationship as a precious plant on the windowsill. It is a plant that someone who loves you very much gave you as a gift. Are you going to say, "Well, this is a very nice, healthy plant, and I'm just going to sit over here and think about it once in awhile but not really put any time or energy into taking care of it?"

No, of course not. Without attention or tender loving care, that plant will wither and die. Even a good, strong, hearty cactus will eventually keel over and bite the dust. Nothing thrives in an atmosphere of neglect. Nothing.

You can't put that plant on your windowsill and come back three months, six months, or even a year later and find a healthy plant thriving there just because you were "busy" or "preoccupied" and not really focused on taking good care of it for that period of time.

If you have a relationship that is precious to you, do everything possible to make the most of it every single day. Tend it, fortify it, nurture it. Give it all the time and attention you can because, as we are growing from day to day, our relationships are either "thriving" or "dying" in the midst of our own personal growth. They don't remain the same. It's up to each and every one of us to see that our relationships maintain strength and good health as we gravitate and grow toward the future.

If you are in a relationship that isn't what it used to be, ask yourself why this is. Did you stop taking care of this relationship, or is your partner at fault? Has one of you quite naturally outgrown your commitment in this relationship or simply chosen to take a new, solitary path for yourself into the future? There are no guarantees in life, only "promise" in terms of what has yet to come. If you can hold fast to this promise, the potential for a happy, fulfilling life shared together alive, you have won half the battle already. When you share the same goal and are deeply committed to it, nothing will ever possess enough power to divide you. Nothing. No temporary lapse in fidelity, no financial problems, or a lack of passion and intensity will do this.

When both partners are truly committed, they have the power to weather every storm. They will lavish attention on that plant on the windowsill and they will tend to it even during the dim days of winter or if it has suddenly fallen to the floor and been bruised.

Some people cannot make the most of their love lives because they simply haven't got one. They need to take a good, hard look at the way they're living their lives in general. Nobody is going to ride up to your door on a white charger to romantically whisk you off for a lifetime of love and happiness unless you happen to be a character in a Disney movie. Even then, your chances might be a little remote. If "Beauty" had left the house, for example, would she have met her true love, the "Beast"? I, for one, sincerely doubt it.

Face it; you have to expand your social circle. You've got to consider your friendships with members of the opposite sex as potential romantic partners. There is no better foundation in the world for marriage than genuine, honest friendship.

You also have to consider how others perceive the way you live your life. If you go out and present yourself as available to anyone who happens to look your way, chances are that real love will be hard to come by. Nobody wants what everybody else can have. Nobody sees sincerity and honesty in someone who falls in "love" every other week. Nobody puts genuine faith in someone who has no faith in himself or herself.

Making the most of our love lives is essentially centered on making the most of "whom" we are and "where" we are in terms of our life paths and our own individual capacities to love. We are always changing, always becoming. This one fact of life will always be so. But if we can view our loving relationships as doing the same with every breath we take, we will become more empowered in the process of loving and more committed to keeping these relationships alive and thriving. We will be more willing to literally "make the most" of the love lives we have while living right now, in the present.

Ten Intuitive Lessons for Women Trying to Understand Men in Relationships

After two decades of reading cards involving relationships with men, I urge female recipients to try to understand the following about the opposite sex on the intuitive level:

1. Men, especially those who aren't in touch with their emotional sides, tend to be notoriously poor at acknowledging their feelings, especially when they feel pressured by a partner completely focused on achieving results where the relationship itself is

concerned. The more an immediate response is pursued from such men, the more I've perceived they feel compelled to pull away from the relationship in general and run like crazy to avoid further involvement. Intuitively speaking, women tend to be far different emotionally. When we are pressured for an emotional response by our partners, the more we feel compelled to step up to the plate, not only voicing, but whole-heartedly committing ourselves to our true feelings.

2. The less "needy" and "victimized" by a man's choices about his life in the present we appear to be, taking a strong posture with him by letting him know that we support him to do what he needs to do to get his life straight within himself, the more we keep the door open for this relationship to flourish in the future, and it usually always will.

3. When we try to do all the right things to the very best of our ability in terms of coping with a difficult relationship but get very little emotionally in the process, pain is the obvious return for us on the investment. My perception is that while we can genuinely try to be patient, understanding, tolerant, forgiving – all the qualities a man needs from a mate in order to bring true happiness and completeness to his life, we can't make him more emotionally available until he is ready to receive these gifts from us.

4. When a man appears in a reading as sharply focused on his own deep sense of emotional frustration, it's rarely the partner causing him to feel so frustrated about Life and Love. He, realistically, only has himself to hold responsible for purposely denying himself the chance to feel the beautiful joy to be gained from both, simply because he refuses to risk opening himself up long enough to experience that joy. Until he is ready to undertake and complete his own personal journey toward such an emotional awakening, we cannot take him further than he is prepared to go in a relationship.

5. We are following a correct path toward the future when we allow a married man in our lives the time and space he needs to

resolve family matters at home and the many emotional conflicts he struggles to conquer within himself. A married man sincerely seeking a new beginning needs his time and personal space, so that he can re-enter our lives whole in mind, body and spirit, rather than as one frustrated and emotionally-compromised, bringing with him "baggage" from having felt pulled so strongly in opposite emotional directions.

6. A man currently in the stage of trying to placate a difficult situation in his life, convincing himself that he can endure without his own needs properly satisfied, is realistically only lying to no one but himself. Men in such situations inevitably become their own worst enemies by distancing themselves from their deepest emotions, believing it is more practical and far easier to simply do their best to "get by" and be complacent from day to day, denying their own intense need to feel loved. These men eventually discover they can only "get by" for so long a time. The directions their lives take toward the future teach them many important lessons in the process. As a man's personal situation continues to erode, it's just a matter of time before he realizes where his heart truly lies and the gravity of the need to be loved, despite how strenuously he has denied this need within himself.

7. Some of the best learning in our lives as women and what we genuinely desire for our futures comes from our own personal wisdom. Men, on the other hand, tend to learn the hard way from experience by making emotional mistakes in terms of their most precious relationships. We are far wiser than we may give ourselves credit for when we allow such men the freedom to leave us and make these mistakes, engaging in new relationships with other women, learning crucial lessons for the future in the process from them. More times than not, we will find these men standing on our proverbial doorsteps at some future point as a result of these emotional mistakes made in the past, yearning to rekindle the relationships with us they once shared.

8. Men tend to put a great deal of energy into talking themselves out of a future they've emotionally entertained with us when conflict

suddenly arises. The memory of that relationship, however, will linger and haunt these men for quite some time to come. But until these men are ready to take that step toward a committed future shared, all we realistically can do is give them the time they need to come to grips with their own emotional insecurities.

9. In general, men are not by nature, likely to thrust someone from their lives unless a situation becomes completely intolerable or the heat of the moment compels them to do so. They tend, instead, to be argumentative and difficult to deal with, hoping an undesirable partner will choose to take flight to alleviate any personal responsibility on their part for the disintegration of the relationship. In readings these men are often perceived to be with entirely wrong partners. My perception is that these men know on a deep, personal level that these relationships will never work with the women in their lives, and it is only a matter of time before such a woman gathers her things and heads for the door. I urge anyone interested in a man already involved with someone else to play it light with him, no pursuing. When he wants to share disgruntled feelings over the woman currently in his life, try your best to be unbiased in the opinions you share with him. The more supportive and caring you can offer yourself up to be with this man, the more drawn he will inevitably become emotionally toward you.

10. When a man has suddenly become distant in a new relationship, often it is because he is exercising caution where the woman in his life is concerned, afraid as a result of something she's said or done to indicate that she might move on in favor of a relationship with another man from her past who could re-enter her life and wish to re-unite with her. Rather than face rejection, he is attempting to protect himself from developing deeper feelings for her, which is really quite foolish in the respect that in his heart of hearts, he knows she is the woman who truly has the capability to love him the way he wants and needs to be loved. Such a man clearly needs the time and space to become surer of himself and the relationship in general.

Intuitively speaking, men often run from love because they feel they are helpless, at a serious disadvantage, incapable of controlling their own futures in the process of Loving. A tremendous amount of this mind set, relates to their own pre-conceived emotional disabilities as partners attempting to engage in wholly committed relationships. These men want to feel that, no matter what; they are still complete men, still very much in control of their lives. Many haven't, as yet, achieved the right emotional level to understand that by opening themselves up to the risk of giving love, they also become strong enough to receive love. In time, they do reach such a level. When they do, they unequivocally realize that the true sense of Completeness they yearn for in life comes from such selfless giving and the strength to genuinely receive love in return.

Finding Love and Happiness within the Framework of Your Life

Personal Prophesy centers on choice and change as powerful instruments to help us achieve a greater sense of happiness and stronger loving relationships within the framework of our own lives.

You might be wondering, What in the world is the "framework of my own life?" In terms of Personal Prophesy philosophy, the framework of your life is its own sum total at any given moment. It is very much like your very own personal stage where your life is taking place in the present as if it were a play, often with, and other times without your own conscious participation.

Sometimes you are on that stage, actively interacting with the others on the stage, causing the scenes to change. Sometimes you are sitting in the audience as a passive observer, merely watching the drama on that stage as it develops and unfolds, with no control over it. Whichever role you play where your own personal "stage" is concerned, intuitively speaking, is essentially up to you more often than you might imagine.

Consider that you can choose to be an active participant in your life by exercising choice in order to bring about productive change, by being in command of your choices and while doing so, effectively directing the majority of the action that occurs on that stage. Or you can choose to be a passive observer in terms of your life by sitting in the audience and allowing yourself to be basically at the mercy of the choices those in your life are making – choices you can only react to –inevitably affecting the outcome of the production (your life) taking place on that stage as you are experiencing it.

Consider the shape and substance of your own life right now. How many of you so often sigh, "I wish I had a better job," but fail to make the choice to aggressively seek one out? You allow yourselves to sit and suffer a dissatisfying career while waiting for your superiors to decide to give you a better job or, in some instances, give you your walking papers. You are just essentially waiting for change to propel you toward a new future, one you could choose with purpose for yourself.

How many of you wail, "I wish I had a better marriage!" allowing your marriages to wither and die over the course of time. This is because you fail to choose to do what you can to make those marriages better as you sit mired in your own complacency. When those marriages end, you let change once again haphazardly point you toward the future.

How many say, "I can't find the right partner to share a meaningful relationship with," and then continue to engage in a series of ill-fated relationships with all the wrong partners. This occurs because we are so fearful of actually taking a stand where our hearts are concerned by choosing to be alone and waiting for a genuinely compatible partner to enter our lives. Instead, we put ourselves at the mercy of incompatible partners and suffer when these partners leave us. Again, allowing change to completely dominate our emotional lives.

As Personal Prophesy teaches us, our lives don't have to be that way. Once we choose not to take a passive role where our lives are concerned and we choose instead to put ourselves in command of it – not so much "reacting" as we are "acting" on our own needs and desires – we literally make the choice to achieve a happier, more satisfying future for ourselves.

Now, of course, just choosing to find better jobs, to make our marriages better, or to seek only compatible partners for ourselves won't suddenly "make" these things happen. But they do have a far better chance for becoming reality within the framework of our lives once we've consciously made the choice to shift our life paths away from the dissatisfaction and fear we feel in the present toward powerful, productive change. Change which, in essence, only makes us that much more receptive to experiencing genuine happiness and fulfillment for ourselves in the future.

Intuitively speaking, that shift becomes an extremely dynamic one once we exercise choice in order to bring about change. We become much more open to opportunity as a result. We have a clearer perception of "who" we are and "what" we want for ourselves in terms of the future, choosing not to accept anything less. We aren't afraid to risk change because we know that by choosing change, we actually put ourselves in command of it.

Choice and change become constructive instruments when you are able to see them for what they are: tools with the capability of guiding you toward a happier, more productive, much more fulfilling future to ultimately enjoy for yourself.

Those who fear change refuse to utilize the power of choice and end up finding that their own lives have been entirely shaped by the choices of others. The framework of their lives is a "stage" they have no control over as they basically sit in the audience and react to what they experience.

The focus of Personal Prophesy is to make you feel much more empowered because you have the tools with which to navigate the future, essentially putting yourself in charge of the action taking place on that "stage." In other words, this is the framework of your life – a production no one can realistically direct but *you*.

Finding True Love

Dianne, a long-term client of mine in her late thirties, recently celebrated her fifth anniversary. The fifth anniversary of her own personal quest to find the man of her dreams, that is.

According to her calculations, she has thus far dated 12 military men, nine police officers, five fireman, three pilots and two lawyers over the course of those years. Yes, you could say Dianne has a thing for men in uniform. (The lawyers were just flukes, she insists, having succumbed to a momentary weakness for blond, muscular, devilishly-handsome men in three-piece suits while getting her will drawn up and the fine print of a real estate contract translated, respectively.)

Despite her best efforts to make these men fit her lifestyle and emotional nature like a kid glove, she still has yet to find Him: Her prince, her knight in shining armor, the man destined to be The One who will enable her to be blissfully happy and feel complete forever.

No matter how hard I try to convince Dianne that what she seeks cannot be found, the more determined she is to prove me and the card readings I give her wrong. In frantic haste, she scours the night-clubs, the vastness of the Internet. She peruses personal ads and peers with anticipation into the face of every new male who saunters into the ad agency where she works. She's certain he's out there. It's just a matter of finding him.

So far, as a result of her romances with these 31 men, she's managed to eat in every expensive restaurant in town, see every famous comedian who headlines at the local comedy club, traveled to exotic islands, met ten different extended families in ten different states scattered across the country. She's even eaten sushi, despite how much she hates fish, twice. All for the sake of finding that one True Love, which she believes, will magically transform her life into a satisfying, deliriously happy existence. Tragically, every last one of these romances has, in one fashion or another, only managed to break her heart.

What Dianne fails to understand – along with a good three-quarters of the human race just as caught up in feverish pursuit of attaining True Love – is that this most lasting, purest, soul-deep kind of Love cannot be "found." True Love "finds" us. When we least expect it. Usually when we aren't wearing our best outfits with our hair perfect and our makeup on. At times when we aren't the least bit interested in loving or being loved. Especially when we're urgently trying to make a relationship with someone we're involved with somehow work, even when we know down deep inside it isn't the right relationship for us in the first place.

True Love simply "happens" *if* we are willing to wait for it. By waiting, I mean, consciously abandoning the urge to go out and purposefully hunt it down. Focusing entirely on our lives, as they exist in the Present, developing ourselves, emotionally and spiritually, to be the best that we can be. Living exclusively in The Moment – the here and now – while concentrating on reaping deep maturity and wisdom from that moment. By facing our own intense fears and successfully conquering them. By relying completely on our own faith that when the time is right, True Love will indeed find us. When it does, that love will naturally fit like a glove. It will seem so right from the instant it unfolds that it might very well scare the be Jesus out of you.

It's the kind of spiritual and emotional meshing depicted, through the ages, in movies, classic literature, paintings, and sculpture. It is so pure and complete in and of itself that it effortlessly transcends every difficulty, every hardship. It heals and restores. It brings joy and beauty to every aspect of our lives. It's the bonding of two souls that nothing and no one can ever divide or conquer.

First... we have to be willing to wait for True Love and have faith that it will arrive. If we aren't willing to wait or we lack the right amount of faith, of course, we can still find love: Romantic Love, Sexual Love, and Platonic Love. Dianne found all three by dating 31 men in five years. Still, she was left wanting that "something more" and ended up getting hurt, despite how the readings she received urged her not to make emotional investments in these men, trying desperately as she was to somehow make what were essentially all the wrong relationships, right.

How can you bring True Love into your life? First, stop looking. Stop pursuing that elusive "someone" who has you so caught up in believing he or she has somehow captured your heart through the cat-and-mouse game of shallow romantic/sexual desire. By all means, stop trying to make current relationships work that simply don't mesh and basically don't hold the potential for becoming reality in the way of true, lasting love for you in the future.

The cards have told me for years that as soon as we stop trying to make true love happen, it will. As soon as we sincerely abandon our search for that Mr. or Ms. Right, the man or woman we are destined to partner with and spend a lifetime with will quite naturally enter our lives. The question is, can you wait and have faith that mate will come for you? Yes, of course, you can.

If you key in on your own intuitive voice, you'll know from that first or second meeting, certainly by the time you engage in that first conflict and see the true essence of the person you are getting involved with that this is not the right mate for you.

If you heed this voice, you'll see these relationships for what they are: significant learning experiences intended to guide you toward greater insight and wisdom about yourself, enabling you to make better, more satisfying emotional choices for yourself in the future.

Above all else, concentrate on conquering emotional fear. We're all afraid of something emotionally, whether it's being alone, feeling unloved, taking the risk of getting hurt. We tend to escape these fears by filling our lives up with a heavy social calendar, an intense work schedule, engaging in meaningless affairs. In some cases, making a hobby out of excessive drinking or drug-taking.

Why put yourself at the mercy of such escape mechanisms? Instead, take a courageous stand with your life. Make up your mind to stop escaping. Consciously commit yourself to facing yourself and your own worst fears. Once you do, the sense of personal empowerment you'll come to feel will be nearly overwhelming.

Perhaps most importantly, focus on having enough faith to open yourself to the immense opportunity the Universe offers you.

A scary proposition? Sure, it is. To say, "I'm going to let go, allowing Life to bring to me what it thinks I need, in its own time, in its own way, as I face my loneliness and pain, rather than dashing out to try to make Love happen on my own," is a scary proposition, indeed.

By committing yourself to this statement, you are, in essence, allowing yourself to leap the great abyss of your own emotional insecurities. From that leap, comes nothing but sheer spiritual strength.

Once you've achieved that strength, True Love is sure to find you!
Love Vs. Obsession

Love vs. Obsession ... Are you possibly "Loving too much?"

In the years I've spent perceiving the future from playing cards, I've seen in the cards that a substantial number of the romantic relationships are those in which an individual is either desperately trying to get someone to love them or they are desperately attempting to keep the love of a partner by focusing all of their attention on them. In both cases, what I am essentially perceiving is "obsession." Neither of these, realistically speaking, has a thing to do with genuine love.

When we obsess over our emotions, we are, intuitively speaking, expressing ourselves on an extremely selfish level. We aren't "loving" those we have feelings for because we want them to be happy, even if it means they choose to live those lives without us. The kind of "loving" we're focused on expressing is basically designed to make *us* happy by doing everything we possibly can to get these individuals to share their lives exclusively with us. And we will often go to some extraordinary lengths in order to try to make that happen.

We romantically chase, pursue – at times, even physically stalk – those we profess to "love." When we engage in relationships with new partners, we tend to be so possessive in our manner of "loving" that they inevitably run for the door to escape what they perceive to be an extremely oppressive and, essentially, unloving atmosphere. When they leave us, we continue to chase them and may even harass them with phone calls and letters. We appear at their doors at all hours of the day and night. We confront their new partners in jealous rages, intent on venting our emotions while making their lives miserable in the process. We may attempt to ruin their careers, their reputations and the families of the objects of our affections. We might go so far as entertaining fantasies of killing the one we profess to love in order to prevent him or her from sharing a life with someone else.

This is not loving. On the intuitive level, this is emotional obsession in its most negative and destructive form, and it is so far removed from genuine love that we might as well call it outright hatred.

When we genuinely give love to others, we selflessly put their happiness ahead of our own. We feel their pains, their sorrows, and we respect their right to freedom, if they should choose to exercise that right. We extend ourselves beyond our own wants and needs to encourage our partners to enjoy rich, full lives for themselves – risking the possibility that we won't be active participants in their lives in the future. We want these individuals to be truly happy as they live their lives – with or without us – because we are capable of truly loving them just that much.

Falling in love, however, is an entirely different story. When we "fall in love," we are experiencing the magnetism of sexual attraction at its most powerful level. We literally feel the urge to mate and be coupled with that individual. This magnetism is an initial stage of loving, but it is far from being its final and most meaningful one. Falling in love only draws us toward an individual with whom we may develop a relationship in the future, but the future depth and substance of that relationship won't have a thing to do with sexual attraction experienced in the here and now.

Consider that when we fall in love we feel entranced, dazzled, and downright captivated with that individual who attracts us so intensely. We feel drawn, consciously or not, to selfishly gratify a deep, inner longing for physical unity with another who characterizes an ideal mating partner for us at that particular time. There's no denying our basic nature to be sexual beings, no matter how technologically advanced civilization may have become. Human beings are drawn to one another essentially to mate, propagate, and, in general, proliferate the species. It's basic human nature, after all.

Loving, on the other hand, is an entirely unselfish act in emotionally extending ourselves beyond our wants and needs. Through loving we recognize that a loved one is a wholly separate person who is traveling his or her own individual path in life without our needing or requiring them to be there for us at any given moment.

When we say, "I can't live without this person in my life," we aren't expressing love but instead, extreme dependency on another individual. We are obsessed and parasitic in the way we feel about that individual. We have focused the essence of our lives on the lives of our partners and are basically feeding off them as they pursue their own happiness in life.

We virtually have no identity for ourselves when we live this way. We are so focused on that partner and what he or she does in an attempt to be happy that we have no idea what it means to make ourselves happy. We are, plainly speaking, living our lives through the lives of others, which is a very unhealthy way to live. Genuine love will never grow from such an unhealthy way of life. only greater dependency and deeper unhappiness is fostered in the end.

If you worry that you might be obsessing rather than truly loving your partner, ask yourself these questions:

1. Are you afraid to allow the one you love the space and freedom in which to pursue his or her own goals and dreams to grow and develop as a wholly separate individual?
2. Do you respect the privacy of the one you love, or do you feel so insecure about the relationship you share that you feel driven to be a participant in every facet of their lives?
3. Are you overly suspicious of your partner's relationships with others – family members, co-workers, and friends – and scheme to destroy these relationships so he or she will ultimately "belong" only to you?
4. Does the thought of your partner leaving you fill you with such terror that you think, "I can't ever let that happen"?

I urge those who are yearning to better understand the difference between genuine love and obsession to pick up a copy of *The Road Less Traveled* by M. Scott Peck, MD. This book directly parallels the teachings of Personal Prophesy in terms of what constitutes truly healthy, loving relationships.

Relationship Addiction

Many of us are relationship-junkies and may not even be aware of it. All we know is that we desperately feel driven to "have somebody" in our lives in order to experience the security that we are loved at any given moment.

Don't feel bad if you are one of these people. You are desperately searching to feel loved within the context of a romantic relationship while searching for a sense of identity for yourself with someone else after another relationship meets a painful end. There are more of us in the world than you might possibly imagine.

From the years I have spent conducting intuitive card readings for others, I'm convinced that more than half of the human race feels driven to find somebody – anybody – who might somehow fill that intense emotional void they feel inside. In readings, these people resemble the prince who went from door to door in the classic Cinderella story to find the foot that would fit the glass slipper. As long as somebody out there can wiggle a foot into that emotional "slipper," relationship junkies are happy.

They travel the nightclub circuit. They scour the personal ads. They relentlessly surf the Internet. These people have but one thought focused in their minds as they conduct their search: to find that "somebody" who will love them and hopefully make them feel complete. This is because they are that lonely and needy in terms of the lives they are living.

I hate to burst your bubble filled with hope and reassurance if you are one of those people. What you must consider, intuitively speaking is that anyone who leaps from relationship to relationship seeking that "I am loved" feeling is only settling for a "quick fix" in terms of loneliness and neediness. They are essentially only kidding themselves in the end.

Real love isn't something you can go out and shop for, like a new set of china. Love just naturally develops in its own way, in its own time. But relationship junkies don't feel they have time to wait patiently for the real thing to come along. They are in constant pursuit of new partners for themselves and at all costs will seek one out – essentially taking whatever they can get in the way of a new partner. As long as that proverbial foot fits the "slipper" they are carrying, they feel temporarily satisfied, perhaps even relieved, not to have to face life alone any longer.

Take a good, hard look at your own past, relationship-wise. Did you honestly allow yourself enough time to resolve relationships in the past and heal yourself before you sought new ones? If you can honestly say you did, and if you honestly took the time to face life alone, dealing with your sorrow and pain before you even thought of undertaking a relationship with someone new, chances are very good that you are secure within yourself. You are not a relationship junkie at heart at all.

A relationship junkie can't take the risk of too much time spent alone. Finding that next partner is not only a preoccupation, but also an intense personal hobby – and why? Not having a partner means that people must develop an identity of their own and cope with their own deep sense of loneliness and insecurity. This can be a fate worse than death to the true relationship junkie.

Realistically speaking, relationship junkies have no identity of their own. They essentially live their lives through their partner's. They need a partner desperately. Being alone is such a scary proposition that they will avoid it at all costs, looking for that "relationship fix" anywhere that they can find it. What inevitably happens?

Relationship junkies find themselves racking up multiple marriages and divorces over the course of time, or they engage in so many committed relationships that they can't even define the word "commitment" anymore.

Love essentially becomes a revolving door to these people that they are either going "in" or coming "out" of, but as long as they feel they are going back "in" with a new partner in the near future, they feel a sense of security. They have also achieved a sense of personal identity.

Whenever I find myself reading the cards for relationship junkies, the solution to their "in" and "out-ness" where love is concerned is as plain as day. It's defined as "spending time alone." Yes, that big, scary word, *alone.*

Relationship junkies are no different from alcoholics and drug addicts in terms of the cards. They are dependent on relationships to such an extent that they think they cannot survive without them. They will do whatever they have to in order to be in them. They will forsake everything else in order to feed the dependency and urgency they feel for a relationship to define their existence. They feel an extreme sense of desperation when they don't get the "fix" they need.

Yet, when a relationship junkie one day says, "No more unhealthy relationships for me," healing has the opportunity to take shape in their lives as the result of such a courageous move toward the future. By choosing not to seek a new partner merely because he or she is afraid to experience life alone, new emotional and spiritual growth can occur.

As painful as it may be initially, they begin to focus more on themselves and achieve a better sense of understanding what their true needs are in terms of a relationship. They become more selective, because they have had the opportunity to become stronger and more secure in their own identity of themselves. They don't feel as driven to engage in any relationship that happens to "fit the slipper" as they are to sincerely commit themselves to a relationship of genuine depth and substance.

You don't have to be a relationship junkie if you honestly don't want to be. It's simply a matter of making up your mind to live with yourself while learning to love yourself without a partner. This will only empower you and make you a much more genuinely loving partner in terms of future relationships, in the end. When you are ready to stop reaching for that quick "fix," here are some tips to help guide you toward recovery from relationship addiction:

1. Look yourself straight in the eye in the mirror and make the commitment to yourself: "I'm not going to date anyone for at least the next six months." Then force yourself to live up to that commitment, at all costs.

2. Face your own worst enemy: It is the fear of being alone. But you must actually spend time alone. If you feel like crying your heart out every night for the first three nights, go ahead and cry. Pace the floors. Rant and rave out loud with yourself. Call a good friend and wallow in self-pity. Grieve, get angry, pray – but no matter what, hang tough on that commitment.

3. Remember that, intuitively speaking, you are breaking a chain in your life that has always compelled you to seek a new relationship in order to feel "safe." Breaking emotional chains is never easy, but by facing the fear of being alone, you allow your own inner strength to grow, putting you on the path toward ultimately conquering that fear, forever.

Keeping Marriage and Long-Term Relationships "Sexy"

Sexual attraction may bring two people together, but sexual attraction certainly won't keep them together. Marriages and long-term relationships will only last when they have been built on a solid foundation of compatibility and friendship.

If you're married or have committed yourself to a relationship based entirely on great sex, all I can say is: boy, are you in trouble. Eventually, you have to get out of bed and cope with the rest of the world. And the rest of the world will inevitably put all sorts of stress and demands on your relationship, which will cause the sexiness in it to fluctuate considerably.

Face it; bills and debt are not sexy. Long hours on the job can make us too tired for all that Olympic sex we used to enjoy. Having kids can take the spontaneity out of passion literally for *years*! This is where having something else going for ourselves, like true compatibility and the understanding naturally attached to it, makes these rough, very un-sexy periods in our lives easier to cope with as we search for ways to achieve passion in our relationships once again.

Keeping your marriage or relationship sexy isn't really all that difficult. It doesn't mean you have to become kinky or far-fetched in the lengths you must go to in order to reach heights of ecstasy after years of living together. You don't have to scream and shout that you need attention if your relationship has started off on the right foot, and you are willing to show consideration and compassion for one another when passion between you fluctuates.

Essentially, it's about putting in the time and making the effort to keep yourselves sexy for each other in some very basic ways. Here are the things I've learned after all the years I've been studying Personal Prophesy, the method I use for perceiving the future from ordinary playing cards.

1. Keep yourself looking just as good today as you did before you walked down the aisle together "way back when." This isn't just a tip for the ladies, but you guys out there especially need to pay attention to this. I'm not suggesting that you have to look like movie stars 24 hours a day, but we could all do better in the appearance department to be more visually pleasing to the partners we love and have committed ourselves to.

2. Put serious effort into staying in the same physical shape you were in prior to committing yourself to this relationship. Strive to stay in shape, to dress attractively, and to practice good hygiene (guys) at the end of your work day. It's too easy to get lazy about dressing well, and to let yourself go weight-wise, to think appearance isn't that important. It is important. Looking good makes your partner see you as an attractive, sexy, and arousing mate. Arousal is just as crucial to the sexiness in your relationship outside of the bedroom as it is in it.

3. Make an agreement that your bedroom is your own personal Garden of Eden where arguments, kid problems, bills, family battles, are not allowed. When you go to bed, tell yourself you are going to bed with your lover, not the stressed out, cranky husband or wife who tends to work too many hours, doesn't make enough money, or didn't get the chores done on time. This is the place where the two of you nurture your love, not find new ways to test its endurance.

4. Fantasize with each other! Keep your sexual lives a living, grow-

ing, and beautiful thing between you. Act out fantasy scenarios together, and send fantasy gifts and letters to each other. Strive to keep what brought you together in the beginning a wonderful intimacy that belongs to no one but the two of you.

5. When all else fails during those times when you are both really busy, stressed, or just not spending as much time intimately as you could. It could be something like, "I need 30 or 20 or 10 minutes, dear," meaning, "I need that much of your undivided attention right now to share alone with you." Doing so will help to nurture your relationship during the difficult periods that inevitably plague all long-term relationships.

Yes, there will be ups and downs and periods of fluctuation where sexiness in your relationship is concerned. But, if you work at it and don't allow the rest of the world and it's problems to steal it away from you, you can keep your relationship sexy for years and years to come.

Long Distance Relationships:
A Common Theme on the Internet

It's been my experience, throughout the years I have been conducting readings for others, that of all the relationships people attempt to maintain in their lives, long-distance relationships are certainly some of the most challenging. And when people fail to take a few crucial factors into account, they can often be the most heartbreaking.

Personal Prophesy teaches us that personal growth occurs regardless of whether we are physically close to those we care for or if we are far apart where distance is concerned.

Whether you are aware of it or not, we are all growing and changing every day. In terms of our emotions and the way we view our lives, we are literally becoming "new" individuals every morning when we wake up. This is also true for the rest of the world. In other words, as a result of what you experience and learn from today, "who" you were yesterday is essentially not "who" you will be tomorrow.

We have a tendency to see ourselves as highly unchangeable from day-to-day when, in fact, we and the lives we are living are entirely shaped by change. This occurs every single moment that we are alive.

When we are physically close to the one we care for and have the ability to see that individual every day, personal growth tends to be a gradual and generally comfortable process in regard to change. We are able, quite naturally, to grow and change together, achieving great closeness in many significant ways.

When we are involved with someone at a distance, however, what might be a gradual process where personal growth is concerned tends to seem far more dramatic when we are able to share physical closeness. This is simply because we don't have the luxury of spending time with these individuals on a day-to-day basis. As a result, change tends to seem very unnatural and may even alienate us to a certain extent.

Whenever we engage in long-distance relationships, we find ourselves continually having to re-establish and reaffirm "togetherness" each time we are able to share physical closeness with the one we love. Some people have the ability to thrive on the intensity involved in "stopping" and "starting" again. Whenever these couples are reunited, they find themselves feeling like new lovers again, they enjoy the thrill of getting to know each other again, and they experience a rather euphoric sense of "newness" about the relationship that draws them close every time.

Other couples struggle with a certain amount of difficulty as they search for a sense of constancy in a relationship where, realistically speaking, there is very little. This is due to the distance that happens to be involved. These couples require a considerable amount of reassurance from each other that the relationship is still, in fact, intact. They tend to experience conflict where personal growth is concerned because distance has caused them to grow and change, separately. They feel insecure about the strength of the relationship. They are driven to question it, but they still strive to re-establish closeness.

Of course, there are those couples who simply cannot endure those changes that inevitably result in terms of personal growth in a long-distance relationship and find themselves so constantly riddled with doubt and worry, they feel they have no choice but to end the relationship – if only to escape their own intense insecurities about it.

As you establish long-distance relationships, try to remember that they will be, as any other relationship in your life, constantly affected by change. If you can adapt to these changes and not feel threatened by them, your relationships will become all the stronger and more loving in the long run.

Another factor involved in whether long-distance relationships will ultimately survive or fail is the way in which they begin. When you meet someone online, and a relationship between you begins to develop, that relationship is essentially taking root in an unreal and entirely perfect environment. It is, as perceived in the cards, an experience that is purely psychological.

There is, of course, absolutely nothing wrong with psychological experiences. From it, we can most certainly learn and grow. We may also feel a tremendous amount of emotion in the process as we go about the business of living our individual lives.

You must remember that at least 50 percent of the time these relationships have very little to do with reality. After all, they exist in a perfect environment. Perfection, as you and I both know, will never define a relationship. It's how we positively or negatively attempt to cope with imperfection in our partners that ultimately defines these relationships.

When you meet someone online, or if you correspond with a pen pal, the "medium" itself may seem very intimate. You may find yourself sharing your innermost thoughts, your feelings, and your beliefs about life in general. You may also find yourselves meshing on such a deep level that you feel sure you are destined to share life together.

Meeting in this manner is not the same as, say, standing side by side in the supermarket, droopy-eyed and squeezing grapefruit. It's not as if you were bumping into each other at a club with a length of toilet paper stuck to your shoe. It isn't an experience grounded in reality the way reaching for the same book in the library would be when he is unshaven and you neglected to put on your makeup. The bottom line is that what we experience in a perfect environment will be entirely different from what we experience in one grounded in nothing but sheer reality.

Can long-distance relationships survive and be successful? From my experience with the cards, I would have to say, absolutely. Over the years I have seen many people achieve a tremendous bond in terms of love and intimacy in a permanent sense for the future. These relationships, however, are only successful when they begin in an atmosphere of honesty, faith, and trust. Those people involved are willing to be realistic and recognize that change will play a significant role as these relationships move toward the future.

Married Women and Extra-Marital Affairs

Whenever I receive reading requests from married women who profess to be extremely unhappy in their marriages, initially they tend to utter the same statements to substantiate their own deep feelings of unhappiness:

"My husband doesn't treat me right; he's abusive a lot of the time."

"He isn't the passionate, caring man he used to be."

"He's so involved in his work now, he doesn't give me the attention I need."

I have learned over the years to wait for the other shoe to drop in these requests, which it inevitably does, nine times out of ten by the third sentence: "I've met a man with whom I share a deep connection. I think I'm in love with him and I'm wondering if I should divorce my husband for him."

Married men, on the other hand, typically bring me vastly different requests for readings about their unhappy marriages. They ask:

"Why has my wife changed so much? She doesn't seem to be committed anymore."

"Does she still love me? I don't want to lose her."

"What can I do to save this marriage? She acts like she wants a divorce."

Even though the male of the species has classically been considered to be most prone to engage in extra-marital affairs, my experience with hundreds of readings conducted for unhappily married men and women over the years leads me to think otherwise.

Yes, statistically more men than women reportedly cheat in marriage. Intuitively, I tend to see more frequent episodes of infidelity in readings as disconnected sexual experiences on the part of these men, which, to them, are not affairs per se, essentially because their own emotional sides are not involved.

The cards however show, time and again, that women tend to outgrow their marriages at a far greater rate emotionally than men do. They are the ones who become, more times than not, involved romantically in extra-marital affairs – especially, serious "affairs of the heart." My perception is that women enter marriage expecting the commitment they make to be a living, growing thing between two people, a commitment intended to only become more satisfying and fulfilling as the years go by.

When that sense of real commitment fails to thrive and grow, many women find themselves emotionally led astray, unconsciously receptive to the romantic advances of men outside of their marriages.

I've never been able to fault these women for such emotional receptivity as I've read their cards. It's been clear to me that they simply – even at times, urgently – yearn only to feel genuinely loved as they live their lives.

A large number of husbands, however, tend to enter into marriage as if it were a significant destination that has at long last been reached. It's as if they say to themselves,

"We're happily married; I don't have to work at this relationship any longer."

Not all of them, of course, but enough of them, gauging from the reading requests I've received over the years from men once they become deeply disillusioned about the quality of their marriages. It's been my experience that these men settle into marriage as a comfortable, routine way of life and only reach the point of desiring to put additional effort into making their marriages what they once were happy and thriving, tragically, after it's already perceived to be too late.

Traditionally, society views marriage as life lived in a vacuum where nothing ever changes. Life simply takes a course of mundane routine and "sameness." Intuitively speaking, this is definitely not the case.

Marriages, like human beings, are always changing, always becoming something new for the future with each day that passes. When we aren't getting what we feel we need from our partners or we aren't giving them what they feel they need, over time our own emotional energies inevitably lead us – and our marriages – in entirely new directions where growth is concerned.

In other words, we are either naturally "growing together" or "growing apart" in the process of daily living. The bottom line is, we are experiencing growth, one way or the other.

Women who are highly intuitive by nature realize they are merely reacting to the emotional absence of their mates and tend to "look before they leap" where attraction to another individual is concerned. They take the time to weigh the ramifications of their feelings and the changes which will result in their lives should they act on sudden, impulsive romantic feelings – feelings which hold the potential to undermine and ultimately lead them from their own marital commitments. While they may enjoy the passion of these extra-marital romances, they frequently choose to stay with their marriages and work to make them more satisfying – particularly when the cards reveal that these extra-marital romances realistically will not last.

My perception in readings is that a large number of new potential partners are actually in the initial stages of falling in love with the married women they engage in private relationships with. Some of them prove themselves in readings to be better partners in the long run for these women. Most, however, do not. Perceived in the cards as merely captivated by the intensity and drama attached to such secretive rendezvous and the high intrigue involved, they are not perceived to be able to handle the weight of a long-term relationship once it ventures out into the broad daylight of everyday existence.

Married women who find themselves experiencing sexual attraction and infatuation leading them to engage in extra-marital relationships because they aren't getting what they feel they need in the physical sense from their marriages or they are simply bored with the tedium of marriage, tend to be wiser and exceedingly happier realizing they are reacting to their own boredom through such meaningless sexual encounters for physical satisfaction (as many women are perceived to do). I encourage these wives to turn toward their marriages and strive instead to re-ignite the passion, which once brought them and their husbands together.

Those who are in danger of falling in love with men outside of their marriages, I urge to proceed with caution and make very careful choices for themselves. After all, the decisions we make regarding our marriages (and new partners entering our lives) profoundly affect the stability of our homes and families, as well as the course of our own immediate futures.

As we travel through life, the more we are able to rely on our own intuitive impulses, the more receptive we make ourselves to better decision-making, which will ultimately guide us in our relationships and marriages through difficult, emotionally-challenging times.

Chapter Nineteen
Understanding,
Coping and Attaining

Whenever I perceive in readings sheer, utter misery in the life of a client, there is always a good reason behind it. Most frequently, my perception is that private, unrealized hopes and dreams lie at its core.

These clients may insist they are happy in every sense of the word. They may even vehemently declare that I am completely wrong in my intuitive assumptions about their lives at that moment. Still, they know on a deep personal level that as much as they try to bury themselves in work, social activities, relationships, remaining fixed on tending to the countless details involved in daily living, they cannot hide from such a deep, fundamental truth about themselves. They are, plainly speaking, downright miserable.

As Personal Prophesy philosophy teaches, to suffer a life filled with misery is not genuinely a "life." It is simply day-to-day tolerance of what are realistically perceived to be intolerably unhappy circumstances. Should you experience such misery in your own life, my experience with readings dictates that as soon as you open yourself up to the abundance of opportunity the Universe offers where your most cherished dreams and hopes are kept and nurtured, considerable success and that all-important sense of deep, personal fulfillment will inevitably come your way in the not too distant future.

How do I know this? From the hundreds of readings I've conducted over the past two decades for truly miserable people who chose as a result to undertake a new path to the future for themselves. Men and women who were convinced they were happy on a shallow, one-dimensional plane of existence. Clients who thought they had to settle for such misery in order to get the bills paid, struggling to achieve acceptance with occupations that offered no significant amount of personal satisfaction for them. Clients trying to keep homes and families together by suffering in silence their own bad marriages. Promiscuous clients who thought sleeping around were a good cure-all for the loneliness and pain that plagued them.

Such misery classically perceived in readings doesn't just "go away" once it's been intuitively defined. It lingers and frequently festers within us until we consciously confront it, cope with it, and ultimately take positive steps to resolve it. Whenever the cards indicate a significant amount of misery in a client's life, he or she tends to feel emotionally distanced from friends and relations, living life on an isolated level, which contributes tremendously to that individual's inability to communicate with others, even when they've needed to the most.

Intuitively speaking, such periods of isolation and feeling distanced are vitally important in order to help these clients become more connected to and emotionally in tune with their own, true inner selves.

Why? Because it's through such dark, difficult periods, through such times of overwhelming misery, that we realize how strong we are, how much we intently yearn to be truly happy. Once enlightened, we purposefully shift our life paths in the direction we most earnestly want those lives to travel in terms of the future.

Most clients, I've found, feel they've done their best over the years to follow their own cherished dreams and goals, inevitably abandoning them along the way, resolutely believing it became necessary to pack them away when success didn't loom as readily as they had anticipated on the horizon for them. They fail to realize that they've needed these years spent facing adversity and personal hardship in order to achieve deeper motional and spiritual growth, attaining in the process a higher level for themselves, psychologically and intellectually, to bring their lives into the realm of being that far much more multi-dimensional where their own personal and professional futures are concerned.

Intuitively speaking, these years are crucial in terms of our own experience, leading us to become more committed and focused, separating the 'wheat' from the 'chaff' you might say, as our life paths turn and shift more into the direction of success and personal satisfaction, guiding us to places where we eventually discover our true future actually lies.

Whenever clients express feelings of severe discontent and disillusionment – even to the point of contemplating suicide – my perception is that while all may seem to be lost, they are not without that single, powerful gleam of light: Hope. By taking the step to reach out, their cards reveal that within them hope still burns, intense and steady, to find a way to pursue personal happiness, to achieve their own true capacity for success, to embrace the love and sense of personal completeness they so desperately seek.

Understanding the Power of Forgiveness

It has been my experience in reading cards as long as I have that two of the most difficult words in the English language to say are, "I'm sorry." Ironically, even more difficult to express are three small words, which essentially hold the power to change every circumstance: "I forgive you."

What is it about our humanness that makes it such a challenge for us to unconditionally accept failings in each other as we walk through life? Of course, people we care for are destined to let us down at one time or another. We're bound to just as easily let them down. We are, after all; only human and prone to make mistakes – extremely profound and hurtful mistakes, at times – as we live our lives.

Nobody I've known in all my years of living has ever demonstrated perfect behavior 50 per cent of the time, let alone all the time. Even though we insist that we deeply love and cherish those closest to us, expressing undying devotion to them "no matter what" the

instant one of these individuals disappoints us by carelessly making
extremely poor choices in their relationships with us, what happens?
More times than not, we immediately turn our backs on them. We
send them packing and out the door. We lash out at them by savagely
declaring, "I'll never forgive you! Get out of my life and don't ever
come back!"

Our hurt and anger propel us into making on-the-spot choices,
which may seem appropriate at the time. And yet, intuitively speaking, by reacting this way all we've really managed to do is close a door
– an extremely crucial door – which ultimately holds the power to
lead us toward a new level of emotional and spiritual growth for the
future.

Aside from true, abiding, real Love, nothing comes through in
readings as clear-cut, nor as meaningfully, as feelings of genuine regret
and sorrow. I've yet to conduct a reading for anyone who didn't, at one
point or another, sincerely yearn for forgiveness from a loved one over a
serious mistake in personal judgment made in the past. Whether it was
a betrayal between friends, infidelity on the part of a mate, or a breach
of faith between family members, eventually the need for forgiveness
and redemption simply can't be avoided any longer.

As this need intensifies, urgent phone calls tend to be placed
sometimes in the middle of the night. Letters of apology suddenly
get written. Seemingly out of the blue, you find yourself hearing from
someone you severed ties with, perhaps even years ago, someone who
unexpectedly seeks you out just to say those words: "I'm sorry."

You may think that because this individual who once consciously
made choices which caused you a tremendous amount of pain or
brought you such extreme personal hardship that you have no emotional responsibility to them anymore. You may smugly think, "See, I
was right. I knew he/she would eventually be sorry." You might even
coldly and callously believe that their suffering is deserved, reveling
joyously in their despair.

I have news for you. When someone comes to you out of a deep,
personal need for forgiveness and redemption, my experience with
card readings insists that he or she is doing more than simply trying

to make themselves feel better by apologizing for their own hurtful mistakes of the past.

That individual is essentially making you emotionally responsible as a result of that apology, putting you in the position of having to make an appointment with your own future by facing a critical fork in the road: whether to reach out with a new, deeper sense of human understanding achieved through your own personal growth or to remain emotionally stunted, incapable of forgiveness, doomed to continue living a rather shallow and narrow existence for yourself.

Coping with Tragedy

It comes in the middle of the night. The middle of a typical workday. It may even come in the midst of an utterly gorgeous Saturday morning as you lounge indulgently in bed enjoying the tranquility of what should be an otherwise ordinary weekend.

That phone call – the one destined to change everything. A call that instantly drives us to our knees in utter despair when it comes, bringing heart-breaking news of sudden tragedy.

Perhaps a loved one has been killed or critically maimed as the result of a serious accident. Given three months to live due to terminal illness. Suffered severe brain damage during a simple appendectomy. Lost a baby to Sudden Infant Death Syndrome.

The list of unanticipated tragedies we inevitably experience in life runs long. The moment we find ourselves standing in when we receive such unexpected tragic news could quite likely prove to be one of the most challenging moments of our entire lives.

Over the years, I have perceived a tremendous amount of tragedy in readings. I have perceived an equally tremendous amount of joy.

Intuitively speaking, joy and tragedy share a critical common denominator in readings. Both are perceived to be the only true measure of balance in terms of the Universe in its most general terms. Both are interpreted as the only true measure of our own personal growth, emotionally and spiritually, over time as a result of our own experience. I say this because the cards interpret both joy and tragedy in readings as intensely meaningful experiences designed with one purpose: to guide us toward deeper emotional/spiritual strength and wisdom as we live our lives.

You might think, "Joy is easy. It's getting what you want and being able to enjoy it. Tragedy is what's hard. It means real suffering and loss. Pain, heartache. Joy and tragedy can't possibly share anything in common."

Can't they? Consider those you know who have experienced true Joy in their lives, if not even yourself, at one time or another. For instance, the joyous birth of a baby after years of trying to conceive or suffering repeated miscarriages. Joyfully achieving life-long professional goals after years of nearly devastating poverty and hardship. The joy of locating biological parents after years of being tossed from one unloving foster home to another.

True joy in life doesn't come easy. It is usually, as I perceive it in readings, to be the result of years of personal hardship and deep, emotional suffering. And yes, even as the result of tragedy.

Ironically, those I hear from most in need of readings as they cope with tragedy are divorced women who claim in their letters to me to unequivocally despise their ex-spouses. And yet, in the face of sudden tragedy, when an ex suffers a near-fatal accident or a serious physical infirmity, which touches dramatically the lives of these ex-wives, it's amazing how forgiving the majority of their hearts are perceived to immediately become in the process.

It doesn't matter anymore in that moment of shock and despair, how absent ex-partners might have been over the years as their children have grown without them. It doesn't matter how gut wrenching their divorces subsequently turned out to be. All that matters, all that ever seems to matter in such crisis situations, is that life will somehow regain a sense of normalcy and miraculously go on as it did before.

These divorced woman tend to want that sense of normalcy to such an emotional extreme that they yearn with their whole heart and soul for it. Anyone who has ever had to face the possibility of such tremendous loss in the eyes of their children knows that no matter how difficult their relationships might be with their ex's, no matter how many the bitter battles, how few the peaceful truces, their kids will inevitably suffer the deaths of that divorced parent intensely. A suffering which, realistically, lasts for life.

When new partners our ex's commit themselves to try to keep our kids and us from participating in these life-and-death crises, it becomes a searing, heart-shattering experience.

After years of reading cards for women who've stood on both sides of the matrimonial fence in such crisis situations, either as an ex-spouse or as a significant other heading toward marriage, readings have unwaveringly revealed intuitively to these women:

- When it comes to a man's ex-wife, you don't owe her much but you do owe her something. After all, had it not been for the failure of her marriage, you wouldn't have the man who parks his shoes faithfully beside yours under your bed to love and to cherish now. Would it really kill you to be decent and tolerant of her presence during such a time of crisis?

  Readings always urge new partners to show their strength by stepping aside rather than becoming victimized by their own insecurities as they try their hardest to push ex-wives away. It's crucial to allow ex-wives the chance to bring her children forward in what should be a time when family members pull together rather than further apart due to petty resentments and bitterness borne of the past.

  Remember, as long as the offspring of that marriage are alive, your man shares a special bond with his ex. A time of crisis presents a wonderful opportunity for a new beginning for all of you, if you pocket your insecurities and let that new beginning take shape in its own way and time.

- When in doubt, just plain, step out. If you aren't sure what you should do under extreme circumstances – as in the case of a life-and-death event – the cards will tell you to take the path of least resistance by blending beautifully with the scenery at that moment. After all, the relationship your partner shares with his ex doesn't involve you it never did and never will. Show you have enough faith in him by leaving him and his ex to work out, not only their unresolved issues, but also their futures as parents in terms of their children on their own. The closer past partners can get to achieving true peace with their ex's, the better the future will be for you, the kids, everybody in the long run.

- Silence may be golden, but true acceptance and understanding are intuitively perceived to be pure platinum. Face it, love never really dies. Get over the fact that ex-wives came first in the lives of these men and still possess a small piece of the hearts belonging to the men they were once married to. If his ex made mistakes in the past in these marriages, the cards will insist that it's your job, as a new partner, to let these mistakes die their own peaceful death with that divorce decree. The past is no longer relevant. It's where we go from this moment forward, all of us, – especially during life-altering crises – that matters most.

It's been my perception after 20-plus years of reading cards that life-altering crises happen for the following reasons:

1. To lead us toward higher understanding of our own spiritual beliefs.
2. To remind us how fragile life truly is and how important it is to cherish the moments we are given to share with others.
3. To bring us closer in our relationships as family members, in our friendships, in our day-to-day interactions with others.
4. To urge us to put aside petty grievances attached to the past and find that all-important new beginning for the future.
5. To ultimately allow forgiveness to guide us to that new place of beginning.
6. To teach us the meaning of true joy as a result of lessons learned from tragedy.

Sudden tragedy is bound to come and dramatically affect our lives, no matter who we are. It's my belief that the Universe, God, the Life Force, however you personally conceive the Higher Power to be, doesn't intend to bring us anguish and suffering without a purpose.

My perception is that there is perfection and balance to all things. Yes, even in terms of tragedy.

Intuitively speaking, to experience tragedy in our lives is a learning experience, a spiritual and emotional awakening, a critical personal reminder that we are fallible as human beings and yet, emotionally capable of extraordinary gestures generated by sincere compassion, forgiveness and genuine love from our hearts. Yes, even when deep resentment, bitterness and prejudice have driven us worlds-apart in the past.

My perception is that the perfection the Universe seeks as we live our lives from moment to moment is not in how much joy we are able to reap and embrace from our own existence, but rather, how we ultimately react to the hardships and agonies characterized by the tragedies we inevitably encounter in our daily lives.

There is no greater learning experience perceived in readings, no moment nearly as profound nor emotionally and spiritually-filled as the one in which we consciously choose to turn our lives in an entirely new direction as a result of tragedy.

In other words, it's how we process the pain of that moment and attempt to strive toward a new day, a new beginning for ourselves and each other as a result of that pain which ultimately brings healing and sets us on a new path filled with understanding for the future.

Understanding Spirituality from the Intuitive Level

Frequently, I conduct readings for highly-complex, deep-thinking individuals who possess so many personal spiritual gifts, they tend not to understand why the rest of the world doesn't feel the same "expansiveness" or see the endless amount of spiritual possibility and potential attached to the Universe that they do.

Intuitively speaking, those around these clients are perceived to live their lives on a level spiritually (meaning "relating to the spirit as a prime, essential force influencing and guiding thought patterns and perceptions; not traditional religious beliefs typically defined as "spirituality") which isn't as enriched with insight and knowledge, nor as intuitively deep as these clients have achieved within the framework of their own lives.

Sadly, these people are incapable of understanding the paths complex; deeper-thinking individuals are walking with their lives. They tend to draw misinformed assumptions that they are "flaky" or "weird". As a result, these clients often find themselves feeling as if they walk through life alone.

This is definitely not what I perceive about such complex, deep-thinkers in readings I regularly conduct for them. My perception is that these clients have achieved such a strong sense of unity with the Universe and their own Higher Selves that they are inherently quite philosophical and infinitely more in tune than the average person with the processes of life, living and death in general. They are perceived to possess the ability to see beyond the physical world and its limitations, grasping the spiritual lessons involved, even though they may not readily believe that they are.

The cards indicate that they understand the natural flow to Life exceedingly well. Intuitively, they are perceived to be far closer in terms of embracing the essence of God, the Life force, the center of energy, which is the Universe, as a result of their non-traditional views and insights. It is truly one of their strengths, this ability to understand the spiritual lessons attached to situations we all confront on a daily basis, particularly life-and-death circumstances and hardships which would no doubt devastate another living life on a different, less insightful and in tune level of existence.

Clients often express to me how intensely they yearn to develop their own intuitive abilities. This, in my opinion, is an extremely easy task to accomplish, considering that we are all intrinsically highly intuitive beings. It's simply a matter of learning to focus more on our intuitive sides and tuning into The Voice which speaks intuitively to each of us, in order to develop the ability to "see" right to the heart of situations we face and in the process, come to understand them very well from this level.

What follows are the spiritual lessons I've learned over the years by heeding my own intuitive voice:

1. Your concept of "God" may not be the same as my concept of God, but if you consciously open the doors of your own heart and intuitive mind, the essence of God and the Universe (as you conceive each to be) will speak personally and intimately to you.

   I can't tell you the number of times in my own life over the past 20 years when I felt terribly lost, frightened or confused. As soon as I sat quiet and allowed, what I've come to term, "my God voice" the opportunity to speak openly and freely to me, the intuitive guidance I received as a result was indeed accurate, no matter how incredible such guidance seemed at that moment, 100 percent of the time.

2. Death is only a door leading from one level of existence to another. When we dream of those who have experienced death and left the earthly plane, we are spiritually communicating with them on the subconscious level during these dreams. They never leave our lives and stand ready to guide and comfort us from this level.

   Loved ones who have passed away always show themselves as spiritually very close to recipients in their readings. I feel the presence of such loved ones powerfully as I conduct their readings, particularly for those clients still processing deep grief. I've yet to conduct a single reading, after all these years, for a recipient where a loved one from the other side didn't have a personal message to convey from the spiritual level.

3. Your path in life is not my path or anyone else's. The most spiritually damaging step we can take is to criticize, condemn or judge each other as we follow our own individual paths toward greater spiritual growth and wisdom. Rather, we should show each other unconditional patience and understanding every step of the way, remembering that our own blessings in life come from a God or a Universe, which ultimately seeks balance in all things.

In other words, if you taint your own path with negativity, bitterness and lack of forgiveness, you will reap the same tainted gifts toward your own personal hardships as you continue to walk your Walk. If you give generously of yourself to others, you'll be blessed generously in return. Balance is the key word here. What we send out to the Universe in terms of our own energy, emotionally and spiritually, is sure to rebound right back at us as personal lessons that have yet to be learned.

4. No matter how complex Life itself may appear at times, always remember: The secret to true happiness is sheer simplicity. In our thinking, our goals, the way we live our lives.

As we all continue our journeys through Life, it's vital, if not downright crucial, that we try our best to rely on our own intuitive voices to guide us as we confront every obstacle and personal test that happens to come our way.

Think about it: The more receptive we make ourselves to intuitive thought, the more capable we are to receive and embrace endless possibility and potential from the Universe – true blessings, every step of the way – toward personal happiness and spiritual fulfillment, now and in the future.

Chapter Twenty

At a Glance Summary of the Cards' Meanings

The Suit of Hearts

These descriptions are intended to help you generate an image in your own mind of that card's essence. Don't be too locked in on the literal meanings given here, allow yourself to feel the flow of intuitive thought on each.

Ace of Hearts	Signifies the home. The other cards surrounding the Ace of Hearts will show you the other influences surrounding the home.
Two of Hearts	Signifies ambition and personal fulfillment, the feeling of an accomplished personal dream, the sense of having made it. Excellent when joined with career and marriage cards.
Three of Hearts	Signifies sorrow and regret, the feeling of having broken a friend's precious possession. Apologies perceived in the cards will be joined with this card.
Four of Hearts	Signifies jealousy, resentment, and malice. The feeling of anger mixed with pain when someone takes the person you love away.
Five of Hearts	Signifies a gift or compliment, the feeling of receiving a beautiful bouquet of flowers.
Six of Hearts	Signifies great promise. The feeling of a bright and sunny road to the future. Personal and professional relationships that develop into marriages or partnerships with tremendous potential for success.

Seven of Hearts	Signifies genuine friendship, pure platonic love. This card will show you who your true friends are, the ones who will be beside you through thick and thin.
Eight of Hearts	Signifies celebration, the feeling of being at a party, having fun, good times.
Nine of Hearts	The wish card. This card means nothing by itself. The other cards around it will tell whether your wish will be harmful or helpful to you.
Ten of Hearts	Signifies true love, unity. The feeling of love that can last through anything and everything. You know that with this person by your side, you can accomplish anything and overcome all obstacles.
Jack of Hearts	Represents a male, usually with green eyes and dark blond to auburn hair, who is either young in age or young in maturity, but has humanitarian ideals.
Queen of Hearts	Represents a caring, empathetic woman with green eyes and dark blond to auburn hair.
King of Hearts	Represents a man with green eyes and dark blond to auburn hair, who is older in age or older in maturity. Loving, caring, humanitarian.

A Summary of the Suit of Diamonds

These simple descriptions for the Suit of Diamonds are intended to help you generate an image in your own mind... allow yourself to feel the flow of intuitive thought for each card. The Suit of Diamonds represent business and commerce.

Ace of Diamonds	Represents partnership, merger, a very strong union or unity. The card signifies marriage and situations like a marriage, such as a partnership, merger, solid agreement.
Two of Diamonds	Signifies secrets and the feeling of suspicion, as if somebody is hiding something from you behind their back.

Three of Diamonds	Signifies petty, domestic conflicts and signals small disagreements that could escalate into more serious disputes.
Four of Diamonds	Signifies cheating, lies, deception, infidelity.
Five of Diamonds	Indicates news. This card is neutral; it simply means you are going to hear some news. The other cards surrounding it will tell you the nature of that news.
Six of Diamonds	Indicates that a relationship exists. The other cards around this Six of Diamonds will tell you what kind of relationship.
Seven of Diamonds	Signifies scandal, gossip and rumors being circulated.
Eight of Diamonds	Identical to the Six of Diamonds in meaning, it indicates that a relationship exists.
Nine of Diamonds	Signifies uncertainty, a decision about the matter in question has not been made. This card has no negative feelings associated with it, although it can signify that someone is uncertain of their feelings for you.
Ten of Diamonds	Indicates money and financial matters.
Jack of Diamonds	Represents a young, materialistic male.
Queen of Diamonds	Represents a female who enjoys spending, and acquiring possessions.
King of Diamonds	Represents an older male, who may work in finance or who is interested in financial matters and determining value.

Summary of The Suit of Clubs

Clubs face cards are the workers or inventors in life, those who advance society.

Ace of Clubs	Indicates communication: phone calls, letters, online interaction.

Two of Clubs	Indicates minor disappointments where expectations are concerned. "The outcome will not be quite as anticipated."
Three of Clubs	Signifies an event coming right at you, so be prepared. Also duration of time; the number "3" is significant with this card, it can mean 3 hours, 3 days, 3 weeks, 3 months...
Four of Clubs	Signifies misfortune. This card warns of a major setback, an unexpected set of circumstances.
Five of Clubs	Indicates an agreement, contracts, deals, commitments, transactions.
Six of Clubs	Represents effort. It focuses on work or the workplace.
Seven of Clubs	Signifies desire and sexual attraction. This card does not represent affection.
Eight of Clubs	Indicates frustration and impatience.
Nine of Clubs	Signifies indulgence. This card represents drinking, drugs, over-eating, excessive socializing. Also, having a good time, enjoying the company of others in a social atmosphere are its more positive aspects.
Ten of Clubs	Indicates something "official." This card focuses on legalities, government or military matters.
Jack of Clubs	Represents a younger male who is idealistic by nature.
Queen of Clubs	Represents a female who is extremely creative and inventive.
King of Clubs	Represents a male who is older in age or spirit with spontaneous wit and sharp intelligence.

Summary of The Suit of Spades

Ace of Spades	Conclusion, Ending. Or Distance.
Upright	It means a conclusion, an ending, it's over. With the death of circumstances, there is always a new beginning.

Upside down/ reversed	The card is telling you about someone or something at a distance, quite far away. The other cards around it will tell you what is at a distance or what the message is.
Two of Spades	Signifies change of direction or change of course.
Three of Spades	Signifies routine matters and unexpected events. (Like running into somebody at the store you haven't seen for a long time). It is generally a pleasant card and the other cards around it provide the emotion.
Four of Spades	Indicates illness or depression. The card cautions you about ill health and mental state. It's a depressing, gloomy, unhealthy card.
Five of Spades	Signifies anger. A clearing of the air needs to happen for new growth to occur.
Six of Spades	Signifies caution. This card is a warning to proceed slowly, hold back, keep certain emotions in reserve. *Sometimes* it indicates pregnancy.
Seven of Spades	Signifies loss. The feeling your purse is gone, job is gone, or lover is gone. It's gone and this card means the object of your affection is not coming back
Eight of Spades	Signifies tears. The feeling of pity, self-pity, sorrow, and crying cleansing, comforting, healing tears.
Nine of Spades	Signifies grief and anguish. This is the feeling of mourning. The period of longing for what can't be brought back. Unresolved heartaches.
Ten of Spades	Indicates a journey. There are no emotions related to this card, it simply means going out or coming back from a journey.
Jack of Spades	Represents a young male, intellectual rather than emotional in how he views the world. He seeks justice and is judgmental by nature.
Queen of Spades	Represents a woman, mentally sharp and often considered to be aloof and not given to emotional gestures.
King of Spades	Represents a male, older in age or spirit. Trust his guidance, he has insight to help you find direction.

Other O-books of interest

The Bhagavad Gita

ALAN JACOBS

Alan Jacobs has succeeded in revitalising the ancient text of the Bhagavad Gita into a form which reveals the full majesty of this magnificent Hindu scripture, as well as its practical message for today's seekers. His incisive philosophic commentary dusts off all the archaism of 1500 years and restores the text as a transforming instrument pointing the way to Self Realization. – **Cygnus Review.**

9781903816516/1903816513•320pp £12.99 $19.95

Everyday Buddha

A contemporary rendering of the Buddhist classic, the Dhammapada

KARMA YONTEN SENGE (LAWRENCE ELLYARD)

Foreword by His Holiness the 14th Dalai Lama

Excellent. Whether you already have a copy of the Dhammapada or not, I recommend you get this. I congratulate all involved in this project and have put the book on my recommended list. – **Jeremy Ball**, *Nova Magazine*

9781905047307/1905047304•144pp £9.99 $19.95

Good As New

A radical retelling of the scriptures

2nd printing in hardback

A short review cannot begin to persuade readers of the value of this book. Buy it and read it. But only if you are brave enough. – **Renew**

An immensely valuable addition to scriptural understanding and appreciation. – **Methodist Recorder**

9781903816738/1903816734•448pp £19.99 $24.95 cl.
9781905047116/1905047118•448pp £11.99 $19.95 pb.

The Ocean of Wisdom

The most comprehensive compendium of worldly and spiritual wisdom this century

ALAN JACOBS

This anthology of 5,000 passages of spiritual wisdom is an awesome collection of prose and poetry, offering profound truths to everyday guidance. A valuable reference for any writer or historian, but it also makes for a good fireside or bedside book. – **Academy of Religion and Psychical Research**

9781905047079/190504707X•744pp•230x153mm £17.99 $29.95

Popol Vuh: The Sacred Book of the Maya

The Mayan creation story

ALLEN J. CHRISTENSON

The most accurate and comprehensive translation ever produced. His work is an extraordinary masterpiece of scholarly analysis. – **Karen Bassie-Sweet**, University of Calgary.

Clear, vital and entrancingly true...a brilliant exegesis, worthy of the treasure it unpacks. – **David Freidel**, Southern Methodist University

9781903816530/190381653X•320pp•230x153mm £19.95 $29.95

Popol Vuh II

A literal, line by line translation

ALLEN J. CHRISTENSON

A definitive document of rhetorical brilliance. – **Stephen Houston**, Jesse Knight University Professor, Brigham Young University

An invaluable contribution... **Justin Kerr**, author of *The Maya Vase books*.

9781903816578/1903816572•280pp•230x153mm £25.00 $37.50

The Principal Upanishads

ALAN JACOBS

Alan Jacobs has produced yet another literary masterpiece in his transcreation of the 'Principal Upanishads', which together with his 'Bhagavad Gita', aim to convey the nondualist teaching (Advaita Vedanta) of the ancient Indian scriptures as well as explore the author's own poetic expression. – **Paula Marvelly**

9781903816509/1903816505•384pp £12.99 $19.95

The Spiritual Wisdom of Marcus Aurelius
Practical philosophy from an ancient master
ALAN JACOBS

Most translations are literal and arid but Jacobs has paraphrased a selection of the best of Aurelius' meditations so as to give more force to the essential truths of his philosophy. – **The Light**

There's an uncanny appropriateness of this work to current times so this book is bound to resonate with many. – **Wave**

9781903816745/1903816742•260pp £9.99 $14.95

A World Religions Bible
ROBERT VAN DE WEYER

An admirable book to own personally for reflection and meditation, with the possibility of contemplating a different extract a day over an entire year. It is our hope that the use of this splendid anthology will grow. We recommend it to all for their personal enrichment. – **The Friend**

Outstanding collection of religious wisdom...never has so much wisdom been concentrated in such a small space. – **New Age Retailer**

9781903816158/1903816157•432pp•full colour•180x120mm £19.99 $28.95

A Heart for the World
The interfaith alternative
MARCUS BRAYBROOKE

This book is really needed. This is the blueprint. It has to be cherished. Faith in Jesus is not about creeds or homilies. It is a willingness to imitate Christ-as the Hindu guru Gandhi did so well. A must book to buy. – **Peacelinks**, IFOR

9781905047437/1905047436•168pp £12.99 $24.95

Bringing God Back to Earth
JOHN HUNT

Knowledgeable in theology, philosophy, science and history. Time and again it is remarkable how he brings the important issues into relation with one another... thought provoking in almost every sentence, difficult to put down. – **Faith and Freedom**

Absorbing, highly readable, profound and wide ranging. – **The Unitarian**

9781903816813/1903816815•320pp £9.99 $14.95

Christ Across the Ganges
Hindu responses to Jesus
SANDY BHARAT

This is a fascinating and wide-ranging overview of a subject of great importance. It is a must for anyone interested in the history of religious traditions and in the interaction between faiths. – **Marianne Rankin**, Alister Hardy Society

9781846940002/1846940001•224pp•230x153mm £14.99 $29.95

A Global Guide to Interfaith
Reflections from around the world
SANDY AND JAEL BHARAT

For those who are new to interfaith this amazing book will give a wonderful picture of the variety and excitement of this journey of discovery. It tells us something about the world religions, about interfaith history and organizations, how to plan an interfaith meeting and much more – mostly through the words of practitioners. – **Marcus Braybrooke**

9781905047970/1905047975•336pp•230x153mm £19.99 $34.95

The Hindu Christ
Jesus' message through Eastern eyes
JOHN MARTIN SAHAJANANDA

To the conventional theologian steeped in the Judaeo-Christian tradition, this book is challenging and may even be shocking at times. For mature Christians and thinkers from other faiths, it makes its contribution to an emerging Christian theology from the East that brings in a new perspective to Christian thought and vision. – **Westminster Interfaith**

9781905047550/190504755X•128pp £9.99 $19.95

The History of Now
A guide to higher yearnings
ANDY NATHAN

This is all about the spark of optimism that gets us out of bed in the morning, and the different ways it has flared to life during the time of humanity. A "who's who" of the world religions.

9781903816288/1903816289•160pp•250x153mm £9.99

Islam and the West

Inside the mind of God

ROBERT VAN DE WEYER

2nd printing

Argues that though in the sphere of economics and politics relationships between Islam and the West have often been hostile, in the area of ideas and philosophy the two have much in common, indeed are interdependent. A military and financial jihad against global terrorism cannot be won. Bit a jihad for peace can, and will render the first jihad unnecessary.

9781903816141/1903816149•128pp £6.99

Trading Faith

Global religion in an age of rapid change

DAVID HART

Argues boldly that the metaphor of trading provides the most useful model for religious exchanges in a world of rapid change. It is the inspiring biography of an intensely spiritual man with a great sense of humour who has chosen an unusual and courageous religious path. – **Dr Anna King**, Lecturer in Hinduism, University of Winchester

9781905047963/1905047967•260pp £10.99 $24.95

Transcending Terror

A history of our spiritual quest and the challenge of the new millennium

IAN HACKETT

Looks at the history of the major world religions, paying particular to nine great prophets, their teachings and what later generations have made of them. All are presented as stemming from the human quest for truth in every age. – **Westminster Interfaith**

9781903816875/1903816874•320pp £12.99 $19.95

O books

O is a symbol of the world, of oneness and unity. In different cultures it also means the "eye", symbolizing knowledge and insight, and in Old English it means "place of love or home". O books explores the many paths of understanding which different traditions have developed down the ages, particularly those today that express respect for the planet and all of life. In philosophy, metaphysics and aesthetics O as zero relates to infinity, indivisibility and fate. In Zero Books we are developing a list of provocative shorter titles that cross different specializations and challenge conventional academic or majority opinion.

For more information on the full list of over 300 titles please visit our website
www.O-books.net

BOOKS